Islam and Christianity

Crossroads in Faith

A. J. Abraham

Wyndham Hall Press

ISLAM AND CHRISTIANITY
Crossroads in Faith

by

A. J. Abraham
New York Institute of Technology

"Treat the other Man's faith gently;
it is all he has to believe with."

H. S. Hoskins

Library of Congress
Catalog Card Number
86-050582

ISBN   0-932269-95-8

Printed in the United States of America

TABLE OF CONTENTS

DEDICATION

For my wife

Esther

and in memory of my grandparents

Saada Abi-Raad

and

Saada Ibrahim

PREFACE

This study is a product of both a need and a request.

Those of us who have the privilege of teaching comparative Near Eastern religions have known for some time of the need for a basic, simple, text on Christianity and Islam, for undergraduates and graduate students, that would present the beliefs of those two religions as their followers understand them. Many Christians have only a brief or sketchy knowledge of Islam drawn primarily from secondary texts on history and world civilizations. The Moslems, on the other hand, possess an even more rudimentary view of the Christ and Christianity essentially extracted from a few scattered remarks about them in Islam's Holy Book, the Quran. And, lastly, for the non-Christian and non-Moslem students we instruct, there remains a basic need for them to have some knowledge of two of the world's great religions. If this study satisfies one or more of those needs in part, I shall have succeeded in this endeavor.

Some time ago, on different occasions, I was approached by several members of middle eastern associations in the United States to write a brief account of the religions of modern Lebanon that would present those faiths to an American public that is quite unfamiliar with them. Therefore, this work, in part, strives to present the originals of Christianity in its Near Eastern environment, emphasizing the church at Antioch as a major center of early Christian diversity, as well as the rise of Islam and the origins of its many sects.

Lastly, the concluding chapters of this study are designed to show the rich polemical legacy of Lebanon which helped the Maronite church to flourish under an expanding Islamic empire. The last chapter is not a polemic in itself but an attempt to show that the differences between Christianity and Islam are not necessarily substantive but, rather, a product of interpretations. That attitude, called "the Lebanese perspective," generated an atmosphere of tolerance and religious freedom that lasted for centuries, and only recently, it has been upset by outside forces and current events impinging upon that formerly harmonious sectarian state.

i

INTRODUCTION

No sooner had our forebearers emerged from the caves to ponder the world about them and to gaze at the vast sky above them millenniums ago, it can be said that the search for God or the gods began, either out of fear, or the realization that man is not his own supreme lord and master of the universe. To placate the forces about them, or to plead for favors from the great unseen powers, our homo sapien ancestors began what may be properly called religion.

The ancient Greeks created a matrix of faith and reason to search out the mighty force or forces that guided the universe, seeking a "prime mover" or "first cause" to all that followed in the heavens and on Earth. Their great achievements in theological speculation culmminated in some of the well known philosophical proofs for the existence of God, as sanctioned and understood in the Middle Ages and in recent times. It is not our aim, nor do we presume, to debate the wisdom of those great thinkers or their arguments - the Cosmological, the Ontological, the Teleological evidence - or any other proofs of somewhat more recent vintage, for the existence of God. It is enough to note that philosophy in the service of religion had its adherents and detractors or critics for each new idea for the nature and existence of God. It is suffice to say that faith remains integral to believing in God (or gods) and that philosophy's own shortcomings can not remedy that problem for the present. Nevertheless, reason dictates and implies that it is, perhaps, more logical to believe than not to, for modern science, as the handwriting of God, tends to support the idea of pre-existent designer of the universe, rather than a cosmic origin in chaotic evolution. Even positive evolution is only an intermediate state and could be seen as a component and compliment to the design process.

Religion has been an integral, intrinsic, and intuitive part of all great civilizations. And, to some extent, all religions are basically similar, that is they all possess someone or something to believe in, a set of sacred rituals or words to

ii

be used and a way of life or culture to guide the adherent from the cradle to the grave. If we were, however, to classify the great religions of the world into three primary categories we can see some fundamental differences emerge. Some would form ethical philosophies such as Buddhism or Confucianism, making no claim to divine intercession or any scientific evidence for their authority; others are purely mythologies of human construction expressing man's limitless imagination, devoid of scientific or philosopical speculation to back their origins; and, the last group, the religions of Judaism, Christianity, and Islam claim divine origins in revelation and reflect upon philosophy and scientific creation (Cosmology and Biology) as proof of the existence of the Revealer (the designer). The latter successfully challenged the beliefs of their day and generated a morally superior way of life and belief to supersede the virtues of the old ethical philosophies and myths. Thus, they won a world of disciples for their faiths.

In the Western tradition of Judaism, Christianity and Islam, the Revealer, the God of Abraham, the Father who called Jesus His Son, and Allah (the Arabic word for God) is one and the same, with the following characteristics:

1. He is real, not an abstraction of man's imagination or a virtual image of the mind.

2. He is spiritual, that, is metaphysical, possessing a soul.

3. He is a living person with self and universal awareness. He is physical in human form (anthropomorphic) and He created man in His image.

4. He is one and unique, all knowing (Omniscient) and all powerful (Omnipotent) and He has no limitations (infinite).

5. He is the Creator of the universe (by scientific laws which only He may alter, suspend or abrogate), and He transcends (is outside of or distant from) His creation.

6. He is perfect in His justice and goodness and wishes that man will live by His precepts out of free choice. (He is non-coercive.)

In order for man to live in accordance with God's will, He has chosen messengers or prophets in this world. Those men were individuals who acted as mediators and interpreters of God's will. The prophet's mind, discourse and, at times, his whole bodily existence became a path, conduit or way for the Lord's message. The prophets spoke for God in the mode of future predictions and revelations that occurred, sometimes against all odds.

The revelations of the prophets were recorded in the Scriptures (the Holy Writings), the Old Testament (Torah), the New Testament (the Gospels), and the Quran. It is in those Scriptures that man's quest to find and know his God may be best sought, although theology (the logic for believing in God) and Christology (the logic for believing in the divinity of Jesus) remains heavily indebted to the Greek philosopical mind, as does the Scholastic theology (Kalam) of Islam.

This study will concern itself with the revelations of Christianity and Islam, building upon the monotheistic belief of the Hebrew religion. Christian revelation was primarily an outgrowth of the Jewish tradition and prophecy regarding God's Word. It is the manifestation of God's plan for the salvation of the human race, not just the Jewish nation; and it was realized fully and completely in the coming of Jesus Christ. Although Jesus did come into a Jewish milieu, His message transcended its localization to become the message of universal salvation. But first, He had to fulfill the Old Testament prophecy, the presciption for Messiahship, in order to validate His mission.

In Jesus Christ, the Word of God became flesh (as the Son) and, thus, He represents the "summit and fullness of revelation (1)." The kingdom of God can only be fully comprehended in the life and ministry of Christ, for in Christ "the Kingdom of God is present and at work (2)." The Apostles of Christ were then commissioned to spread His message to the rest of mankind, as recorded in the Gospels. He instructed His followers to Baptize all mankind in the name of the Father, the Son and the Holy Spirit (Mt.: 28:16).

The New Testament as a source of revelation was seen by the early Christian community as a new covenant that inherited the old, became superior to it (3), and superseded it, to a considerable extent.

In Islam, the Holy Spirit is identified with the angel Gabriel as the agent of revelation (4), and Muhammad became the last recipient of God's word on Earth, as both prophet and messenger. The Quran uses two distinct terms to express the sacred character if its revelation - the word **wahy** implies "inspiration" (5) in its recipient and the world **tanzil** indicates the "sending down" (6) of a message from heaven. Hence, Revelation in Islam, as interpreted from the Quran, is the descending of the Words of God in an inspired form through Gabriel to the Prophet Muhammad as a guide for the human race. But, what is its relationship to Jewish and Christian revelation?

The Quran speaks of Revelation in a manner that created three great schools of thought on the subject. Firstly, the Quran was transmitted in Arabic, in the Prophet's dialect, to warn his people in the cities about him, and to clarify its (the Quran's) meaning to them (7) (Q 42:7; Q 5:4). Thus, the early Moslem commentators of the Quran believed that the Quaranic message was only for the Arabian community. It was a direct response to Muhammad's quest from his God for a Holy Book to guide his people. Other Quranic phrases imply that Muhammad was not to be an "innovator" bringing a new message (Q 46:9) but, rather, one who "recast the substance of the teachings given to Jews and Christians, perfecting and completing them (8)." That is, the Quran was basically a harmonious synthesis and interpretation of preceeding revelations, having never intended to establish a new or separate religion or to deny the previous revelations. And, lastly, as Islam became a world religion, it is believed today that Islam was initially God's plan for the world (Q 9:32), continuing and completing the process begun by God in the Old Testament, passing through the New Testament, and culminating in the Quran. As evidence for this, Muhammad is said to have written to the world leaders of his time inviting them to submit to his religion (9).

The revelations of Christianity and Islam are intended to set man free from sin, or ethical and moral malpractice. In observing the teachings of the Gospels or the Quran, man can live a life in "God's light," according to "God's will," and thereby inherit a place in "His Kingdom," upon death. Not to obey God's laws is to fall into error. However, God would not enslave His creation and, therefore, man possess freedom of conscience, during one's life.

v

The conditions for sin in both Christianity and Islam are, consequently, similar. One must be aware that they are violating a religious precept; one must commit a sin intentionally, with the aim of harming one's self or someone else; and, lastly, one must believe and understand that they have committed a sin, transgressed the word or law of God. All three conditions must be present for moral guilt to occur and to place the individual outside the community of the faithful, and to subject the person to divine punishment, castigation.

In order to understand one's responsibility towards God, as a Christian or Moslem, it is necessary to study the concepts, themes and motivations of those two great world religions from a historical and literary perspective, and to understand them in a way similar to their early followers.

INTRODUCTION NOTES

1. Rene Latourelle, **Theology of Revelation,** New York: Alba House, St. Paul Publishers, 1966, p. 45.

2. **Ibid.,** p. 52.

3. **Ibid.,** pp. 67-69.

4. J. W. Sweetman, **Islam and Christian Theology,** part 1, vol. 1, London: Lutterworth Press, 1945, pp. 25-29.

5. Fazlur Rahman, **Islam,** Chicago: University of Chicago Press, 1979, p. 31.

6. Fazlur Rahman, **Major Themes of the Quran,** Chicago: Bibliotheca Islamica, 1980, p. 103.

7. G. E. Von Grunebaum, **Medieval Islam,** University of Chicago Press, 1954, p. 76; Tor Andrae, **Muhammad, the Man and His Faith,** N.Y.: Harper Torchbooks, 1960, p. 97.

8. **Ibid.**

9. For the text of the letters sent to the rulers of Egypt, Byzantium, and Persia see: Ahmad abd Al-Ghafour, **Humanism in Islam,** Lebanon: Matb'at al-'Alum, 1980, pp. 62-65.

ONE SOLITARY LIFE

"Here is a man who was born of Jewish parents in an obscure village, the child of a peasant women. He grew up in another obscure village. He worked in a carpenter shop until He was thirty, and then for three years He was an itinerant preacher. He never wrote a book. He never held an office. He never owned a home. He never had a family. He never went to college. He never put His foot inside a big city. He never traveled two hundred miles from the place where He was born. He never did one of the things that usually accompany greatness. He had no credentials but Himself. He had nothing to do with this world except the naked power of His divine manhood. While still a young man, the tide of popular opinion turned against Him. His friends ran away. One of them denied Him. He was turned over to His enemies. He went through the mockery of a trial. He was nailed to a cross between two thieves. His executioners gambled for the only piece of property He had on earth while He was dying - and that was His coat. When He was dead He was taken down and laid in a borrowed grave through the pity of a friend. Nineteen wide centuries have come and gone and today He is the centerpiece of the human race and the leader of the column of progress. I am far within the mark when I say that all the armies that ever marched, and all the navies that were built, and all the parliaments that ever sat, and all the kings that ever reigned, put together have not affected the life of man upon this earth as powerfully as that One Solitary Life..."

Author Unknown

CHAPTER ONE

THE ONLY SON

Jesus of Nazareth, the Messiah, the Christ (Christos) was born in the full light of history, when Rome was master of the known World. The city of His birth was Bethlehem, in the Roman province of Palestine. He lived there for most of His life; He preached, taught, worked miracles, and gained a small following. His short career ended tragically. He was arrested and tried by a Jewish court for blasphemy; He was turned over to Pontius Pilate, the Procurator of Judea, for a second trial as a seditionist. He was condemned to death by the Roman authorities, during the reign of Tiberius Caesar. He was crucified among criminals, on a hill outside the city of Jerusalem. After His death, His followers claimed that they saw Him on numerous occasions; they sat, talked, and ate with Him; and they physically touched Him. Death claimed no victory over Him! His disciples believed that He was the expected Messiah, and the one and only Son of the Living God.

The events described above, the entire life, death and subsequent resurrection of the Christ, were an inconsequential, perhaps even, a trivial occurrence, if seen from the imperial seat of power in Rome. It was a routine execution of a conspirator against the state, or of an agitator in a far flung province of a vast empire. As such, our Roman archives yield little about Jesus of Nazareth and His disciples.

The Roman historians provide us with only a sketchy glimpse of the life of Jesus and the early Christian community. From the writings of Suetonius, **Lives of Twelve Caesars**, the **Letters** of Pliny the Younger, and the **Annals** of Tacitus, it is clear that a man named Jesus was executed near the city of Jerusalem approximately 28 A.D., and that He was the leader of a small band of followers (1).

The Jewish historian Josephus refers to Jesus in his major work, **Antiquities of The Jews,** and in a shorter one entitled, **The**

Jewish War. Of Jesus, he wrote, "It was about that time that a man appeared - if "man" is the right word - who had all the attributes of a man but seemed to be something greater. His actions, certainly, were superhuman...(2)" And, lastly, there are some interpretative references to the founder of the Christian faith in other Jewish sources (3), some quite unflattering at best.

This brief description of the life of Jesus, His execution, and the existence of His disciples is sufficient, however, to enable us to say that Christianity is a historical religion (4). The events in the life of Christ took place in a specific space-time continuum - they are real historical events, they did not take place in a mythical time or location; but rather, they occurred in a historical reality or frame of reference, whose precise dates, however, may not be ascertainable. Nevertheless, the events are real and the locations are identifiable in our world today. The first Christians were Jewish believers in Christ, and as Jews they possessed an aversion to mythology and paganism. They considered the pagan religions and myths to be a variety of useless and meaningless superstitions.

The early followers of Jesus sought to preserve their knowledge of the Christ and His teachings for future generations. Jesus left no written records of His own life or teachings, and it is apparent that the early disciples, His Apostles, believed that He would soon return (His parousia/second coming) after His ascension, some forty days after the resurrection. Consequently, the written records of His life and teachings came many years after the actual events had taken place; they were written between 64 and 105 A.D., when His return was no longer considered imminent. They were recorded in the Gospels (the Good News/Evangelion/Evangelium), also called the New Testament (New Covenant). The Gospels were a proclamation **(kerygma)** of His Messiahship and more; they were written for the existing Christian community as a record for future generations. The Gospels are unique among the Hellenistic literature of their time (5). They had "no model, precedent," or analogous source to follow.

The Gospels were never intended to be copies of one another, and the fact that they differ does not indicate any error in composition. There are four Gospels in the New Testament, attributed to Matthew, Mark, Luke and John. Although they

2

may not have been written by those   men, they bear their names as the source of the revelations. The Gospels are believed to be eye witness accounts that may have been dictated to the actual writers or scribes.

Each of the four Gospels was written for a different community, and that fact bears witness to the differences in style and emphasis. Mark's Gospel is the oldest and, apparently, Matthew and Luke relied upon Mark's account in their Gospels. Those three Gospels are referred to as the Synoptic Gospels for they give a "synoptic view of the life of Jesus (6)," and possess a similar construction, approach, and a "harmony" of sorts. The Gospels of Matthew and Luke also relied upon another source, a collection of the sayings of Jesus called by modern Biblical scholars Q (Quelle/source) (7), possibly written in Greek or repeated in oral form and, then, at a later date, written down. The Gospel of John appers to be an independent construction.

Greek, the languge of the Hellenistic East, was the language of the Gospels. They were written in Koine, the common idiom, easy to understand, clear, and precise. Since each Gospel was written for a different community, they each emphasize or reflect a different historical tradition (8). It is believed that Mark's Gospel was largely written for the non-Jewish (Gentile) population of Rome and its empire. Matthew's Gospel was directed towards the Jewish Christians (Jewish believers in Christ) and for the Gentiles of Asia Minor. Luke's Gospel and the Acts which he authored were addressed to the Roman administration and the educated pagans in the empire. And, John's Gospel seems to have been aimed at the Greek intellectuals, the theologically and philosophically oriented. The Gospels reached out to a wide variety of people (9) emphasizing different events and themes that would be more meaningful to each community.

Appended to the Gospels are the Acts of the Apostles, the Epistles, and the Book of Revelation (The Apocalypse) which together form the complete New Testament (Diatheke). The Acts and Epistles record the early history of the Christian community and the letters and instructions given to the early church to resolve some of the pending problems it faced. The last entry is a prophetic piece of literature with Christ as its central figure, in a newly redeemed world, ushering in the new order or age to come.

3

The central figure of the Christian faith is Jesus of Nazareth. Who was He? What did he teach? The remainder of this chapter will attempt to answer those questions, at least in part.

It is obvious from the Gospel accounts of the life of Jesus that His apostles grew slowly but surely in their knowledge of the Christ, as it was revealed to them, during the brief years of His ministry. The gradual awareness of the Nazarenes' identity did not in any way lead to confusion about who He was but, rather, it was a cumulative process that led them, step-by-step, to an astonishing conclusion. So startling was their final realization that the twelve demoralized Apostles regained and reaffirmed their faith in Him, and set upon a path that would shake the mightiest empire in the world to its very core, and win it for their Lord.

The Gospel writers refer to Jesus of Nazareth in several terms which apparently were quite clear in meaning to them. It must be understood, however, that the twelve Apostles of Jesus were Jewish and saw things from a uniquely Jewish tradition and perspective. They, later, expanded their vision of the Christ to encompass and envelop the pagans who knew little about, and cared less for, Jewish tradition, scripture, law, or beliefs. Their genius lies in their ability to clearly articulate who they believed Jesus to be without compromising their monontheistic beliefs or associating the Christ with any pagan understandings of the terms they used to describe Him.

The Apostles believed their leader to be a new prophet **(nebi)**, one who came in the Jewish tradition of an intercessor between their God and His creation. In reference to Himself, Jesus used the term prophet several times in regard to His mission among His own people, and in the vicinity of Jerusalem (10). That He came in the older line of prophetic succession is also clear from the question He puts to His followers, regarding His identity. Some of them identified Him with the Judaic Prophets of the past - John the Baptist, Elijah, Jeremiah and others (11), but, obviously, always within the prophetic tradition of the Hebrews. This association was a necessary first step for the fulfillment of a more important Jewish prophecy, that of Messiahship.

The proud and glorious civilization of the Jew of antiquity had fallen upon hard times. As the possessors of the only true

4

convenant between God and man, as His people and nation, the Jews believed that as long as they kept the faith of their forefathers, God would work through the nations about them to confuse their enemies and, thus, protect them. The Jews were never capable of accepting the rule of pagans over the nation of God. And, lastly, they blamed themselves for the catastrophe of Roman rule, a consequence of either their lack of faith or their failure to observe the Laws of God (the Mosaic Code). They awaited the coming of a savior, the Messiah, who could have been either a military-political figure capable of fomenting a successful rebellion against Rome or a religious, prophetic, figure who could renew their faith and lead the Jewish nation to salvation from Roman barbarism. The Christ fulfilled the second condition, as the awaited Messiah.

It is obvious that Jesus, as well as many others, was well versed in the Old Testament's prophecies regarding the coming Messiah. In fact, a community of pious Jews waited, in preparation, for the Messiah's appearance. Those Jews had formed the Essene community (12) of which John the Baptist may have been a member. Some scholars believe that Jesus could have lived among the Essenes during the years of His life that are not chronicled in the Gospels. In either case, whether He did or did not live among them is not extremely important for this study. What is important, however, is that there may have been many others who attempted to pose as, or really believed that they were, the Messiah. (None of them successfully pressed their claim.) Thus, even if Jesus had been an Essene, why did He, and He alone, succeed in convincing others that He was the Messiah?

What lends even more credence to the Apostles' claim that Jesus is the Messiah is the apparent fact that both the Jewish and Roman authorities attempted to discredit Him and His Messianic mission, for it was seen by them as a threat. But each obstacle they placed in His path was overcome in a manner that encouraged His followers to believe more strongly in Him as the awaited Messiah. For His Apostles and followers, the obstacles placed in the way of Jesus only served to fulfill the Old Testament prophecies concerning Messiahship. Jesus may have set out to complete the prescription given for the Messiah, but it was, in fact, the Jewish and Roman authorities that made them come true, against their own best interests and their vigorous, utmost, efforts to do the opposite - to cast Him as an unsuccessful pretender to Messiahship.

The Apostles saw in the life of Christ the fulfillment of the prophetic formula for the Messiah (13), if one accepts the premise that the Messiah is an individual, a person, who is to be the suffering servant of the Lord (God). Some Jewish scholars, however, have interpreted the suffering servant to mean the Jewish nation as a whole and, therefore, they have discounted the role of a person in the Messianic hope (14).

The Gospel accounts indicate that Jesus claimed to be the Messiah (15), the Anointed One, that was expected to come. Jesus asked the disciple Peter who he believed He was and Peter affirms His claim to messiahship, a revelation for him. At His trial before the Sanhedrin (the Jewish High Court), Jesus confirms His role as the Messiah, in clear, explicit, terms that his accusers understood.

Jesus used the term Son of Man in self-description, as well That title has several implications (16), the most obvious is its reference to His human nature, or possible in regard to all mankind. As such, the title depicts the humanity of Jesus or identifies Him more fully with the rest of the human race. It is, in that case, a reference to the biological Christ, His human nature. The term is also rendered understandable as a messianic title, in regard to Old Testament literature (17). Jesus used the title in connection with His prophecies, life, death and resurrection, in numerous Gospel passages. It is, in fact, used more often than any other title for the Nazarene.

The Gospels, however, lead us to an even more astonishing understanding of the Christ. Thus far, we have briefly discussed the titles given Jesus in the New Testament by His followers, as they comprehended them or were capable of understanding them, from their own perspective. But, a more startling claim would be made, one that tore the monotheistic Jewish community asunder. That claim was not of human origin, for the newly born Christian commmunity. It was God's own description of Jesus; it was revealed on at least two separate occasions, to His followers. The first incident occurred early in Jesus' career, at His baptism. During that ceremony, Jesus is identified as the Son of God, by God's own voice saying,

6

"This is my beloved Son"/"Thou art my beloved Son." It is both an affirmation of the divinity of Jesus and the Fatherhood of God (18). And, once again, the voice of God would be heard. The second occurrence took place on the Mount of Transfiguration (19); God's voice called out to the Apostles Peter, James and John saying, "This is my beloved Son, with whom I am well pleased..."

The Apostles were, apparently, to reach an even more astounding conclusion that left no doubt in their minds regarding the Messiah's identity. The culmination of the revelations they had been receiving transpired after their discountenance, upon seeing the death of their leader. It came in the most spectacular and peculiar way. Huddled together in fear and frustration after witnessing the crucifixion of Jesus, the Apostles awaited a sign of what was to come. Their master had promised them something, but they could not come to grip its full meaning, as yet. They hid in fear and trepidation but also in hope.

It was then that Jesus appeared to the Apostles, not as an illusion of the mind or some form of hallucination, but in the flesh. The resurrection was not simply a spiritual or mental event but, rather, a biological reality (20). The Gospels record that the Apostle Thomas doubted what he saw until he physically touched the wounds of the risen Christ. The Apostles and followers of Jesus witnessed His bodily resurrection. But, it was Thomas who proclaimed the final revealed truth in saying, "My Lord and My God." This was, and is, the Gospel's inescapable conclusion.

The title Lord **(Kurios)** in the Gospel is a Greek word that has many meanings and uses. The Gospel's use of the word is, however, clearly in the same meaning, sense and intent that it has in the Greek version of the Old Testament (the Septuagint). It was used in that text to refer to Yahweh or Jehovah, the name given to the Hebrew God. In using the term, Thomas establishes the final link in the chain of revelation identifying Jesus of Nazareth clearly, directly and irrevocably with the Lord, the God of Abraham; the Semitic High God; the Lord of the Worlds; the God of the Universe.

The context of the Gospels shows that the titles referred to in the foregoing pages are not titles in the sense of a common usage, such as the terms president, king, doctor, saint or professor. They are neither earned or ascribed titles applied to Jesus but, rather, descriptions of Him. They tell us who He is, in essence and nature, and His "titles" Lord and Son of God are not transferable or applicable to anyone else. They should be understood as they were in the first century A.D., by the Apostles and their disciples. Those men were neither fools or hypocrites; they communicated precisely what they saw and believed. While we may interpret the Gospels as we choose, we cannot lose sight of what they are trying to say, to tell us. Thus, when the Gospels speak of Jesus as the Son of God or the Lord, the Apostles believed that He was unique, not a child of God (in a spiritual or human sense, as we all are) or one of the children of God (meaning a member of the Jewish nation or community, or the children of Israel), but that He was the Son of God, one in being with the Father in Heaven, and, the only one.

Thomas' verbalization of Christianity's fundamental creed was not a matter of a single instantaneous revelation. Jesus had been establishing His claim to divinity throughout His ministry, and He did it in no uncertain terms, so that it would be unmistakably clear to His followers. He guised that identity in phrases that the Jews of antiquity would understand and would not confuse with similar titles of the time, used by non-Jews. That may be precisely why Jesus did not make a simple declarative statement of His divinity such as "I am God," or "I am God's Son," or "I am the Son of God," for those expressions were in common usage at the time by Caesars, Pharoahs, kings and others. Confusion could have arisen between a ruler who took himself seriously to be a god, or the son of such a ruler. The Apostles did not take the claims of those pagans seriously, in fact, no Jew did, but others in the Roman Empire, the non-Jews, were accustomed to those assertions.

It is apparent from the Gospels that Jesus used phrases that established His spiritual identify and divinity using basically Hebraic ideas, and in regard to the God of the Jews, and no other diety. The Gospels inform us that Jesus claimed to exist before the Patriarch Abraham saying that "before Abraham came to be (was), I am." He claimed eternal existence (21). He clarified His position in regard to God, the Father, as well, saying "I and the Father are one," and, "Whoever has seen me has seen the Father," thereby upholding Hebraic monotheism. And, lastly, of Himself, Jesus said, "I am the Resurrection and the Life" using the terms "Resurrection" and "Life" to depict two properties that the Jews believed belonged only to their God. It is true, however, that some people possess the power of life and death over others, as the ancient rulers could order the death of any of their subjects or could release one from the penalty of death. But, only God has the power of resurrection of the dead and eternal life. In this case, Jesus identified Himself with the Pharisee sect of Judaism which believed in the resurrection of the dead. (Jesus also condemned the Pharisees as well. It seems possible that Jesus criticized one branch of that sect, the more orthodox Shammai school, while He may have favored the more liberal Hillel branch.) Nevertheless, Jesus demonstrated His divine power by the resurrection of the dead on several occasions, but particularly in regard to His friend Lazarus who had been dead for several days and had begun to "stinketh" in the grave. Jesus restored life to others as well. In all instances, the actions of Jesus were done by His own power, that is the power contained within Him.

So firmly convinced were the Apostles of the divinity of Jesus that later generations attempted to reject the human nature of Jesus (the biological Christ) as unnecessary or unimportant, while others even denied His physique, altogether.

There is little doubt that Jesus taught in the general pattern of the rabbis of the first century A.D. (22). His Apostles often called Him Rabbi; the method He employed in teaching was the parable, often used by rabbis, to illustrate a principle or to help the listener arrive at a specific conclusion. (In the Gospel of John the allegory, a Greek educational tactic, is used.) The parable is an example used by a teacher, it is non-historical and applicable to present and future circumstances. Its objective is to make a, more or less, general point of view manifest. As such, it is a creation of its author, fictitious in nature and, consequently, that fact lent credence to those who claim that the Gospels are composed of myths. The parables should be understood as examples or stories used like any other illustrative educational device, and not as a special case of myth making. (Even as fiction, the parables and allegories do not affect the historicity of anything else in the Gospels.)

The teachings of Jesus of Nazareth are many, comprehensive, generalized to some extent and, lastly, meaningful for all times, places, and human conditions. They are, in fact, too numerous for even a brief listing here, thus only some of the more important ones will be recalled. Among the basic teachings deduced from the Christ and the Gospels are:

1. The Fatherhood of God and the brotherhood of mankind - humanism of the highest caliber applied to Christian and non-Christian.

2. Jesus taught the repayment of evil with good.

3. He asked his followers to sincerely forgive their enemies and sinners, and even to love them as much as they loved one another and Him.

4. He taught His followers to treat others as they themselves wished to be treated.

5. He condemned hypocrisy, especially in religious matters, as well as the accumulation of wealth resulting from greed.

6. He opposed ceremonialism and the fulfillment of the Law (religious law) as the center or essence of religion, by replacing that center with faith and love. He took the Law into a higher three dimensional sphere consisting of the Word, the mind, and the spirit, thus perfecting it.

7. He favored self-denial to avoid sin; and He favored the repentance of the sinner. (Jesus forgave every manner and nature of transgression if the sinner truly repented.)

8. He spoke of the resurrection of the dead and life in another dimension (heaven), in His father's kingdom.

9. He spoke of the end of this world as we know it, at some imprecise time to come.

10. He taught the true meaning of love, perhaps the most unique aspect of Christianity.

11. And, lastly, He taught His followers to pray and to be baptized. (Jesus had no need for either but, rather, He participated in those events to instruct His disciples.)

Some of the above teachings must be further elaborated or expanded upon because they involve indepth patterns of human behavior. The weak, sick, and helpless are the responsibility of the Christian community, even if the afflicted are not Christians. The poor are God's special concern and although they may be with us forever, their suffering, however, should be lessened; and, the lack of wealth, prestige, or power should not be considered a sign of God's disfavor with anyone, nor should the burden of illness or disease.

Sin was related to poverty and illness in Old Testament times, and only God had the power to forgive sins. For the Christian, sin (23) can result from thoughts or deeds, or the lack of compassion, or the refusal to aid others. Sin is the failure to act according to the faith; it is the inability to respond positively to others. Sin is the failure to show love. Sin is the lack of pity and respect for the less fortunate. It is the rejection of the common humanity of mankind, by indifference. It is a simultaneous act against both God and man. Sin is a denial of God and Jesus Christ. It leads to hypocrisy which is most damned in God's eyes.

That man can fall into sin is only human nature. It must be viewed as part of our universal human existence. Sin can be forgiven, should be forgiven, upon a pledge of redemption and reform by the sinner.

Jesus came into this world to call the sinner back to God and to show that the God of wrath and punishment is also a God of forgiveness (24), for the believer; and, a God of love for His creation. Anything that was base or unclean, Jesus could make noble or clean again. Thus, the teachings of Jesus are totally compatible with human nature; they do not call for the impossible and they make room for the weak among us. The teachings of Christ cause no pain or suffering but, rather, they bring redemption and salvation.

The punishments for sin in the Old Testament are no longer enforceable; stoning for adultery, for example, is inhuman,

11

unjust and far in excess of the guilt. Now, redemption and moral reform are the path to please God, to find favor with Him, and to return to the fold. Jesus entered a community that already believed in God, and those believers even if taken in sin continued to believe in God. The penalties of old, in fulfilling the law, applied to the backslider who was a pagan at heart, not a believer who succumbs to human weakness. Hope is the message of Christ. (Jesus did not intend to ignor the law; He made it more just and gave it new meaning. He freed man from the fear of punishment in belief and gave both saint and sinner the hope of eternal salvation. He made the law more humane.)

Jesus summarized His message in The Sermon On The Mount, by going far beyond the Law to create a new relationship for mankind. He said:

Blessed are those conscious of their spiritual needs, for the kingdom of heaven belongs to them.

Blessed are those who mourn, for they will be comforted.

Blessed are the meek, for they will inherit the Earth.

Blessed are those hungering and thirsting for righteousness, for they will be filled.

Blessed are the merciful, for they will be shown mercy.

Blessed are the peacemakers, for they will be called the children of God.

Blessed are those who have been persecuted for righteousness sake, for the kingdom of heaven belongs to them.

Blessed are you when people reproach you and persecute you and lieingly say every sort of wicked thing against you for my sake.

Rejoice and be glad for great is your reward in heaven.

Blessed are the pure of heart, for they shall see God.

And, He added, later:

Blessed are those who have not seen and believe.

The sermon is simple and clear, yet in its own right, it is profound, for it was love, of God and mankind, that is the cementing force, the fuel, of Christian thought. That love transcended all human bonds and barriers; it summarizes the Savior's faith in the whole human race, without exception.

Saint Paul said it eloquently in his letter to the Galatians. He said, "There is neither Jew nor Greek, there is neither slave nor freedom, there is neither male nor female; for you are all one (person) in union with Jesus Christ." Persecution and prejudice of race, religion, or sex - of every ilk -is stricken dead with that statement and a commitment to Christ, if one truly is a Christian. That is Jesus' gift of love to the human race - absolute freedom and equality within mankind. Freedom and equality is the message of Christ.

Paul tells us that love is patient; love is kind. Love is not jealous, it does not put on airs, it is not snobbish. Love is not rude, it is not self-seeking, it is not prone to anger; neither does it brood over injuries. Love never fails. Love is the message of Christ.

Love is what led Jesus to pay the ultimate price for the sins of man. No one took His life; He gave it freely, out of love for mankind. He proclaimed His own death as part of His eternal mission. It was the conclusive sacrifice, in human agony, so that all who believe in Him may have life everlasting. Jesus paid for the sins of disobedience, the transgression of Adam and Eve, against God the Father, for which man in his inferiority could only make an inadequate compensation, at best. While God did forgive Adam and Eve, the divine dignity of God demanded an appropriate and equal counteraction for absolute justice to prevail; and that required atonement by someone of equal stature to God to remove the sin, the insult, to the divine being. Jesus was the stainless, perfect, sacrifice demanded by God for Himself. Thus, God the Father gave up His Son's life (the Father's own sacrifice as well) for the love of His creation. And, Jesus submitted His life willinging out of love for His Father and the whole human race.

The Cross is the symbol of victory over death and sin. But, its message also represents much more. It is message of the courage, the triumph, and the humanity of Jesus of Nazareth (25). We see His love of mankind in the forgiveness of His tormentors. He is, at all times, at peace with Himself and His enemies. Jesus is the "Prince of Peace." Peace of mind and body is the message of Christ.

Jesus accepts the burden of the Cross voluntarily, free from coercion, for it is not a humiliating death of a prophet or

Messiah, but a victory for God. Jesus made this clear in saying "I lay down my life that I may take it again." Without the resurrection, it would have been an ignoble death. With His death and resurrection, man has a new beginning - atonement completed; the ransom is paid. Mankind has been renewed, revived and redeemed and all can live free from sin, in order to achieve salvation and paradise.

Lastly, we must ask ourselves what is the significance of the bodily death of Jesus. Could God not have achieved the same objectives and results otherwise, since He has the power to do all things? If so, why did God, the Holy Spirit, become man, inhabit the body of Jesus, in the Incarnation. Firstly, Jesus had to live as a full and complete human to demonstrate that His teachings could be followed by mortals, thereby ending, once and for all, the excuse that the laws of God could not be followed by mere men. Jesus would be the model human for the human race. And, He also wished to draw mankind closer to Him by participating in our humanity. Secondly, there were many people in the ancient world who ridiculed the belief in gods, saying that the prophets were mad men hearing voices in their minds. The philosophical skeptics only believed in what they could touch and see. The Incarnation was the strongest evidence, proof, for the existence of God, in a skeptical world. The nascent Christian community saw their God and testified to it, unto death itself. Lastly, until the coming of Christ both Jews and pagans held a highly negative view of the human body. The Greek philosophers, in particular, believed it was a hindrance and embarassment to man, a prison for the soul. It was the instrument for human sexuality without love, for lust and individual pleasure. In Jesus, the naked human body is sanctified, no longer an object of shame, guilt or embarassment; no longer an object for amusement, recreation, or suffering in the Roman Circus. Love in the male-female relationship changed human sexuality from vice to affection, to caring, and to devotion, not a mere contractual agreement.

Then, the bodily resurrection came three days after the crucifixion, showing that death is an empty victory, as empty as the tomb (a cave) into which the body of Christ was placed. It convinced His Apostles that the impossible task that He gave them was possible. The disheartened, frightened, men were transformed into a dynamic force that could not be stopped. They were filled with joy, in seeing the risen Christ.

Happiness is the message of Christ. The Apostles were transformed by their faith and happiness; they were convinced that Jesus had died and was now alive. He remained with them for forty days and He was seen by scores of people. And, when He departed from our world, Jesus promised them He would always be with them whenever they gathered in His name, and that the Holy Spirit would guide the Apostles in all that they would do. He promised to return, once again. Until then, Jesus passed the message of faith on to them. Faith is the message of Christ. In His own words, Jesus had said it many times. "Your faith has saved you."

Jesus left mankind with a precious gift and an eternal inheritance, yet unmatched by anyone or anything since then. He said, "whoever believes in me will live even though he dies, and whoever lives and believes in me will never die."

CHAPTER ONE NOTES

1. Howard Clark Kee, **Jesus in History**, 2nd ed., N.Y.: Harcourt, Brace, Jovanovich, 1977, pp. 45-48; F. E. Peters, **The Harvest of Hellenism**, N.Y.: Simon and Schuster, 1970, p. 481.

2. Taken from Josephus, **The Jewish War**, England: Penguin Books, 1972, pp. 398-400.

3. Kee, **op. cit.**, pp. 48-54.

4. Huston Smith, **The Religions of Man**, N.Y.: Harper and Row, 1958, p. 301.

5. Kee, **op. cit.**, p. 139.

6. Peters, **op. cit.**, 484.

7. For a detailed discussion of the Q source see: Kee, **op. cit.**, pp. 76-120.

8. See Paul Tillich, **A History of Christian Thought**, N.Y.: Simon and Schuster, 1968, pp. 1-16 for an excellent background sketch of the origins of Christianity.

15

9. Kee, **op. cit.**, Chapters 4, 5, 6 and 7 give additional implications of the Gospel message and the audience to whom they were addressed.

10. William Barclay, **The Mind of Jesus**, N.Y.: Harper and Row, 1976, pp. 132-133.

11. **Ibid.**, p. 171.

12. On this community see: Peters, **Harvest...**, pp. 638-640.

13. A brief comparative analysis of the Old Testament text and the Gospels' text yields the following paradigm on Messiahship:

1.	Psalms 2:7; 22:13-19 110:1	John 3:16-17; Luke 23:33 Mark 16:19
2.	Genesis 49:10	Hebrews 7:14
3.	Micah 5:1-2	Matthew 2:1-6
4.	Isaiah 53:5, 8; 7:14; 9:16	1 Cor. 15:3, 4: Luke 1:32, 33
5.	Zechariah 9:9	Matthew 21:5
6.	Daniel 9:24-26	Galatians 4:4
7.	Deuteronomy 18:15, 18, 19	John 7:40-46

1) Messiah as the Son of God, to die by a method of crucifixion, and to sit at the hand of God.

2) Messiah born into the tribe of Judah.

3. Messiah eternal and born in Bethlehem.

4) Messiah is a descendant of David and is to die for the sins of His people.

5) Messiah is to enter Jerusalem.

6) Time of the Messiah's arrival.

7) Messiah is to be a prophet.

14. For the opposite point of view, see: Arthur W. Kac, **The Messianic Hope**, Michigan: Canon Press, 1975, pp. 57-118.

15. Barclay, **op. cit.**, pp. 172, 227.

16. **Ibid.**, pp. 141-149.

17. **Ibid.**, pp. 142, 144-145.

18. **Ibid.**, pp. 27-29.

19. **Ibid.** pp. 177-182.

20. **Ibid.** p. 301.

21. Kee, **op. cit.** p. 233.

22. Peters, **op. cit.** p. 485.

23. This paragraph is reconstructed from: Barclay, **op. cit.**, pp. 121-128.

24. **Ibid.** p. 109

25. **Ibid.** p. 109.

25. **Ibid.** Chapters 26 and 27.

CHAPTER TWO

THE COMMISSION

It all began in Roman Palestine; it all began in Judea. It all began in the vicinity of Jerusalem. It began with a commission given by the resurrected Christ to His Apostles commanding them to go forth and Baptize all mankind in the name of the Father, the Son and the Holy Spirit; and to make His name known to the World. The missionary movement in Christianity began with the twelve Apostles and St. Paul (Saul of Tarsus, of the tribe of Benjamin). It carried the Good News (the Gospels) of Jesus of Nazareth in to the Grecco-Roman World and well beyond, but, first, it began with the church of Jerusalem. By the end of the first century A.D., Christianity had bridged the gap between Hebrew tradition and Greek philosophy, with its preoccupation with "being," its creeds, and its dogmas. Traveling further West, into the Roman World, Christianity impacted upon and absorbed the Roman tradition of law emphasizing ethics, morals, and human nature. By the second century A.D., Christianity had established a very solid foundation to build upon, and world-wide potential.

Not much is known about the early church in Jerusalem; what we do know is that it became increasingly untenable in the face of hostility by the Roman administration and the Jewish authorities. Of the original twelve Apostles, Simon (Peter), Andrew, James, John, Philip, Matthew, Bartholomew, Thomas, James (the son of Alphaeus), Thaddaeus, Simon (the Canaanite) and Judas Iscariot, even less is known. (Judas committed suicide and was succeeded by Matthias, according to the Acts.) Those men continued to worship at the local synagogues and preached among the Hebrew community whom they believed to be their first priority and primary responsibility (1).

The going was rough. James was the first to officially head the Jerusalem commmunity. His tenure, however, was cut short, for he was martyred, being stoned and clubbed to death in Jerusalem in the year 62 A.D. (2). Thus, James, "the

18

Righteous," the first Bishop of Jerusalem, died in service to his Lord. He was succeeded by Simon since the Apostle John had departed having become a companion to St. Peter (3). As for the remainig Apostles, with the notable exceptions of Peter, Paul, Bartholomew, and, later, Luke, less is known.

It is believed that Thomas took the message of the Lord to Persia and India; Andrew to the Scythians of southern Russia; Philip died in Phrygia; and John in Ephesus. The later Apostle Mark is associated with Egyptian Christianity and the North African church; James with Compostella in Spain; and Joseph of Arimathea with Gastonbury. However legendary these accounts may be, a dispersion of the Jerusalem church did take place, spreading the Christian faith far beyond its original confines (4).

Within Jerusalem, the Christian community established the first (universal) church (**ekklesia/ekklesia katholike**). The departure of Peter, and later John, had left James in charge of the nascent Christian community. A committee of seven (5) men were chosen or appointed to direct the social activities of the new church, since it was being increasingly isolated from the social life of the Jewish community. And, new converts to the faith from the Hellenized Jewish groups outside Jerusalem had put a tremendous strain on the center of Judaism. Those Hellenized Jews were part of the Diaspora and as such their perspective had changed under the influence of Hellenistic philosophy. Stephen appealed to them directly by preaching in their synogogues and, then, he proceeded to attack the Law and the Temple, replacing both with belief in Christ, as the center of a redeemed Jewish faith. He was called upon to respond to the charges against him before the Sanhedrin and, shortly afterward, Stephen was stoned to death in 34 A.D. (6). The climate in Jerusalem became enflamed; the future of the church was in grave danger.

The initiative remained with the Temple authorities. The new "heretical" sect of Judaism had to be extinguished before it took firm root among the Hellenized Jews. One person was particularly, specifically well suited for the task, a high educated Hellenized Jew, Saul of Tarsus (a city of Cilicia).

The spread of Christianity into Syria and Cilicia provoked the Jewish authorities in Jerusalem to send for that famous

19

student of Rabbi Gamaliel, to crush the movement among the Hellenized Jews of the east (7). Saul was a Roman citizen (he inherited citizenship). He spoke Greek and Aramaic as well as Hebrew, and he studied Judaic Law under the renowned Gamaliel, Like his teacher, Saul was a Pharisee (8), convinced of the perfection and completion of the law. He had studied Greek philosophy and the oriental religions of the East. Saul was, without a doubt, perfectly suited for the task set before him. His abiding hatred for those who minimized or rejected the law was clear from this role in the death of Stephen. Saul had proven to be an energetic defender of (orthodox) Judaism.

With the threat to Judaism subsiding in Jerusalem, Saul was assigned the task of rooting out and destroying the new heresy in the East. According to his biography in the New Testament, Saul was traveling toward Damascus when he was striken blind, but, first he saw the image of Christ before him asking him why he had persecuted Him. The voice ordered Saul to complete his journey. (Saul's companions heard only the voice in the wilderness.) During his stay in Damascus, Saul was visited by a leader of the new sect, a man named Ananias, who instructed him in the teachings of Jesus and, apparently, Baptized him, giving him the name Paul. He saw the light of day again.

Paul became an eloquent and articulate disciple of the Christ. He was, in fact, so persuasive in his preaching that a plot was hatched to kill him. But, fortunately, he escaped from the city at night, having been lowered over its wall in a basket. He, then, made his way back to Jerusalem. From there, Paul carried the message of Christ into the major cities of the empire, in the East.

The defection of Paul was Judaism's greatest loss. For Paul, the Incarnation was the "final revelation," the end of the divine plan for salvation "from all eternity" to the present (9). But, it was still largely a Jewish phenomenon, not clearly understandable to the rational "Greek" mind. That bridge had to be crossed, and it was, in the Syrian city of Antioch.

Antioch, lying north-east of Damascus on the Orentes River, was the third largest city in the Roman East. It had a sophisticated and diverse population, representing a wide variety of beliefs and practices (10). Among the pagan population, the Hellenized Jews had assimilated Greek ideas but rejected the pagan religions which they saw as nothing more than "evil" cults (11). The pagans, themselves, had begun to regard their myths with suspicion and skepticism; they were old and tired beliefs that yielded nothing; the old gods no longer satisfied the rational Greek mind. Among the educated elite, the myths were being ridiculed, but, nevertheless, they were engrained into the cultural and social life of the city. They had become habits, customs or popular cults, but could no longer answer any important questions about life, its purpose, its meaning or its origins. Mythology was dying slowly but surely. In its place the Greek mind had discovered the logos ("logic").

The Greek term "logos" means "word" or "reason." But it has many other meanings (12) besides the literal one. It had come to imply the "ultimate rational principle regulating the universe"; "the will of God"; "the universal law of reality" ("the law that determines the movements of all reality"); for the Stoics, "it was divine power," or "the divine seed"; and for other, "moral law," or "theoretical reason," and, finally, the "self-manifestation of god," and His "work."

The term became associated with the Jewish scholar Philo Judaeus and his systematic theology, in an attempt to apply philosophical rationality to Jewish thought. The next step was to apply the logos to Christian concepts. That was, perhaps, the major contribution of the Apostle John and his Gospel.

Clearly, John specifically set forth to utilize the idea of the logos in his writings which were directed toward the theologically and philosophically sophisticated readers in the Roman Empire. For John, the logos takes on a specific meaning. It is the divine purpose in both the creation and the redemption of the world; the logos is both God and Christ, co-eternal. The logos is the "Word" (the reason) become flesh in Jesus Christ - it is the Incarnation (13). In John's own words, he begins his narrative saying, "In the beginning was the Word," (Logos) "and the Word was God"...and..."was made flesh, and dwelt among us" (as Christ). Thus, John facilitated the understanding and conversion of the non-Jewish communities to the Christian faith, in terms they could more easily understand. By adopting Philo's concept of the logos to the life of Christ (14), John succeeded in opening the door of

Christianity to the Gentiles. But the door was not wide open, as yet. Other issues had to be reconciled or resolved first.

At Antioch, Peter was the first bishop and this was the church's second Apostolic See (15). Peter's activities there were a bit obscure, but his prominence had been well established, for Jesus had entrusted the future of the church to him (16). The early church traced Peter's authority to Christ's command giving that apostle the "keys to His kingdom." The church, however, could not locate Peter easily as he wandered throughout a vast empire and, apparently, as the church spread from its nucleus in Jerusalem, it underwent a new top level organization.

Both Apostolic succession and a highly organized church date from the earliest beginnings of Christianity. The simple home meeting place provided the much needed secrecy and, with that, security, for the nascent church, surrounded by a hostile world; but, within the church itself, there emerged three distinctive orders (17). Early in their travels, Peter, Paul and James saw the need for organization in the church. At Jerusalem, a body of elders (**presbyteroi**) assisted Peter, James and John. In their travels, Paul and Barnabus appointed elders or overseers (**episkopoi**/bishops) who acted as the presbyters had done and who were aided by a deconate (**diakonos**).

Church membership was, however, the key issue that plagued the church. How should a non-Jew (Hellenized or otherwise) become a Christian. The issue raged within Antioch and also between the Christian leadership there and in Jerusalem, and it centered around two key problems. The first is whether or not the new male candidate for the faith should be circumcized and the second involved the eating of food sacrificed, or dedicated, to the pagan gods (idols). These issues revolved about an even larger issue - observance of the Judaic Law. The church hierarchy split on these questions as did the Antiochian community (18). There emerged four specific groups ranging from the need to observe both circumcision and the law, to only the need for the dietary laws, to those who saw no need for either one and, finally, those who saw no need to associate Jewish cult practices or festivals with the new community (the separatists) (19). Paul and his friend Barnabas together with the support of Peter favored a Gentile Christianity with Baptism replacing circumcision and the dietary

22

laws; James and the Jerusalem church did not. In the end, Paul's group won (20) and he became the "Apostle to the Gentiles." Food sacrificed to pagan gods, however, was still forbidden to Christians and, thus, a compromise ensued.

In the long run, the Jerusalem church declined in power and some of its early followers disbanded, after the execution of James. Many of the remaining Hebrew believers in Christ were thought to have traveled east to Syria, where they became known as the Ebionites or they could have become a new sect called the Nazaraeans (21). They were eventually accused of heresy in not accepting the virgin birth of Jesus (22). The once proud church of Jerusalem fell into semi-obscurity between 80-85 A.D., with anathematization by the Synagogue: "May the Nazaraeans and heretics be suddenly destroyed and removed from the Book of Life (23)." Apparently, they were, but the church did survive, and it flourished in Antioch where the name Christian was first given to the followers of Jesus, both Jew and Gentile alike.

During the Apostolic Age (the first two-thirds of the first century) and the Sub-Apostolic Age (the last one-third of the first century) (24), the church settled down, as the Apostles and their new converts traveled about the empire making additional converts from among all ranks, races and classes. They were rapidly becoming a social force that the Roman authorities had to contend with, but internal dissension was visible, as well. This development was not unexpected (25) and, perhaps, it was the Apostles' rationale for the centralization of the teaching authority of the church in the episcopate and the Holy Sees. The Gospel's warn their readers of false prophets, apostles and teachers to come (26). As long as Peter and Paul were alive, however, the church had recourse to their counsel.

In the Apostolic age, the existence of Peter and Paul are well illuminted. Peter's life was one of suffering, arrest, trial and a miraculous escape from Herod Agrippa's prison. He traveled to Antioch and Corinth and, finally, he undertook the seemingly impossible task of carrying the Good News of Jesus of Nazareth into the heart of the Roman Empire. Peter is credited with the founding of the Universal (Catholic) Church there; his impact must have been great, perhaps, enormous, for the Roman authorities feared his infectious message. He was arrested and, soon afterwards, Peter suffered martyrdom, being crucified head down, for he believed that he was unworthy of dying in a manner similar to his Lord. He perished during the Neroian persecution in 64 A.D. Paul's career also ended on a sharp note.

Paul's life mirrors that of Peter's. He extended the message of Christ throughout the eastern world, preaching and teaching in Cyprus, Asia Minor, Ephesus, and Corinth. He was arrested in Jerusalem, imprisoned, and tried. Paul was then sent from Caesarea to Rome on a galley which became shipwrecked; he found himself in Malta, having survived that catastrophy. A few months later, Paul set sail for Naples and, later, he arrived in Rome. He resumed his task of teaching and preaching but soon ran afoul of the Roman authorities. As a citizen of Rome, he was tried and, consequently, suffered extinction (27), by the Roman executioner's axe. It is believed that Paul died by decapitation, according to tradition.

The lives of the Apostles Peter and Paul were filled with heroism, courage and unbounded faith. When they worked miracles, they did so in the name of Jesus Christ and by His power alone. Their martyrdom, therefore, should not be regarded as a failure of sorts but, rather, as a "spiritual victory," by laying down their lives for their Lord, who had given His life for them and all mankind.

With the Apostles gone from the historic scene, the church (the Christian community) had to rely more heavily upon the Gospels. Mark, a disciple of Peter, noted down Peter's teachings for his Gospel, shortly after Peter's demise. Luke and Matthew drew upon that account (28), to produce their "eye-witness based" works. Thus, Mark's Gospel was the earliest Gospel (70 A.D.), while Matthew produced his Gosepl in Syria, probably at Antioch, between 80-90 A.D. (29). Matthew's Gospel reflects the church's problems in Antioch and the Christian moral tradition that had developed in an apparent vacuum from the Jewish church at Jerusalem (30).

The four Gospels are not complete biographies of the life of Christ, although they contain much biographical information and material. Apparently, it was only natural for the followers of Jesus to want to know more about His life, and this led to the rise of numerous gospel accounts or tracts. Many were produced, some well into the Middle Ages. But only the four accounts attributed to the Apostles Matthew, Mark, Luke and John, the Acts, the Letters, and in the east, the Apocalypse of John, were fully accepted by the early church as canonical, for having "an authentic apostolic base" and a degree of "reliability (31)." The contents of other historic fragments may have contained some valid oral traditions about the life of Christ, but verification problems led to their exclusion, for heightened accuracy. The Gnostic Gospels which circulated in the Near East were likewise rejected, although they claim to possess "hidden" or "secret" knowledge given by Christ to His Apostles, beyond what was already given by Him to them as insights (32). None of those non-canonical Gospels were adopted by the church; only the well established writings were approved to form the orthodox texts of the New Testament (33). A problem of exclusion had to be dealt with also. What value or role should the Christian church assign to the Old Testament, in its literature.

A controversy arose over the issue of including the Old Testament with the Gospels. Maricon, an analytical writer and a bishop's son from Asia Minor, believed that the Old Testament was no longer central to the Gospels (34). He wrote a major work entitled **Antitheses** in which he contrasted the God of the Old Testament, as God of law, vengeance, and wrath, with the God of the New Testament, as a God of love, mercy and compassion; and he rejected the importance of the birth and childhood of Jesus (35). The church rejected Maricon's philosophy upholding the Old Testament as a preface or introduction to the coming of Christ and the New Testament and, therefore, a compromise occurred. For all the church's effort to obtain a high degree of uniformity in the Gospel tradition, not much can be shown, for heresies based upon the interpretations of the sacred text soon appeared.

The heresies were many and could be found throughout the Roman Empire, particularly in North Africa and in the Near East. In this study, we are concerned with those that flourished in the east, specifically those affecting the church of Antioch. Therefore, we shall refer only briefly to the Church Fathers and the Christian community of North Africa.

From Egypt, Christianity spread towards the major cities and centers of North Africa. The Coptic church of Egypt (36), founded by the Apostle Mark, flourished and Alexandria became a vibrant intellectual center of the expanding church. Among the Latin Fathers of the North African church are Tertullian, Cyprian, Jerome and Augustine. Jerome was the first person, it is believed, to have translated the Bible into Latin (the Vulgate). And, Augustine wrote the famous **Confessions** and **The City of Gold** which became two classics of early Christian prose. Clement of Rome (190-203 A.D.) harmonized Helenistic culture with Christian beliefs and Origen (211-232 A.D.) wrote an allegorical interpretation of the Bible. Other defenders of the church include Justin of Samaria, Tatian the Syrian, Athenagoras the Greek and Theophilus, Bishop of Antioch. (Those men were all Hellenizers of the second century A.D. who sought to give the church a renewed meaning while expressing their diverse ethnic backgrounds and heritage.)

During the early persecutions of the North African church an attempt was made to collect and destroy all Christian writings. In the fourth century, Donatus, one of the bishops of Carthage, refused to surrender his holy texts to the pagans. He maintained that to do so was apostasy. His followers, who were also disciples of Cyprian, Tertullian's student, broke from the universal church maintaining that their own sacraments were valid. That validity depended upon the "the proper standing of the ministers." The Catholic response was that the sacraments could not be polluted by the status of the priest or anyone else (37). Pope Stephen's position, in 256 A.D., was that the sacraments belong to Christ, not the minister; and the Council of Arles (314 A.D.) upheld that view (38). The sacraments - Baptism, Confirmation, Holy Eucharist, Penance, Anointing the sick, Holy Orders and Matrimony, to use their modern names - were all visible in the early church. They were understood then as they are now as certain acts or actions that were instituted by Christ or administered to Him, in the establishment of His ministry on Earth. As such, they are extremely important, sacred, and directly traceable to the Gospels. Of course, they differed in form and presentation from place to place, and time to time, yet they were considered indispensable, as part of the works and teachings of Christ, in primitive Christianity (39). Baptism was practiced as it was in Judaism and the Eucharist (**Eucharistia**) was reminiscent of the Last Supper of the Lord (40), distributed either before or after the main meal of the day.

26

Other heresies emerged regarding the person of Christ, His divine and human natures. Those controversies led to major Christological doctrines that infected the entire east. They are too numerous to be fully discussed here, however, the major disputes that impacted upon the Eastern Church will be briefly mentioned. Those contentions may be categorized into three primary groups: the Monarchists, the Docetists, and the Monophysites. There was also a claim to a new prophetic tradition which, in effect, challenged the growth and dominance of the Apostolic tradition, and the role of the bishops.

Montanism (41), a heresy of the last third of the first Christian century, was based upon the claim of Montanus to "private" revelation, depicting himself as the Paraclete. He claimed prophethood and a new tradition aimed against the "worldly church"; and with the support of two followers, Pricilla and Maximilla, he became a major "disruptive" force to the church hierarchy. He and his movement were condemned by a Synod of Bishops for blasphemy against the Holy Spirit, the one and only true Paraclete. (Other interpretations of the Paraclete as an individual include mediator, helper, friend, consoler and defender; but, the Christian Paraclete is a divine person or manifestation of divinity, first as the Christ and then as the Holy Spirit.) The above incident, however, served a higher objective, that is, it established the Church Councils (the Synods) as the final arbitrator of church doctrine.

The bishops, however, were not always in complete agreement. Paul of Samosata, a bishop of Antioch, began a Christological dispute among the church hierarchy (42). Paul believed that Jesus was one in will and love with the Father and, only later, He received the Holy Spirit to become divine. For Paul, the Logos of John and the Holy Spirit were not persons but, rather, eternal powers and forces that were "qualities of God." The church Synod of 286 A.D., held in Antioch, condemned the Samosataian and his views for declining the logos from being "substantially" in the body of Christ, from His conception.

The logos continued to plague the church leaders and it spawned a variety of beliefs that can be treated under the general subtitle of Monarchianism (43). The Monarchists doctrine bears a heavy tint of Judaic monotheism applied to the logos as the Father, Son and Holy Spirit. The name implies the unity and majesty of the Hebrew God, but the thoughts reflect a Hellenic or

Hellenistic understanding. The Monarchian doctrine criticized the Logos of John's Gospel preferring to have, in a general way, "God the Father on Earth" as Jesus Christ. This school of thought proliferated into Modalism (in which Father, Son and Holy Spirit are modes of the same being); Sabellianism (founded by Sabellius who said that the Father, Son and Holy Spirit are the same divine reality using different "names," "manifestations," "faces," or "appearances," but they are not truly three beings); Emanationists (who implied that Jesus emanated from the Father, as are all things); and, lastly, the Adoptionists (who believed that Jesus was filled by the logos (as the Holy Spirit) and, therefore, He was adopted as God's Son.) In all its diverse forms, Monarchism did not deny the divinity of Jesus but, rather, it attempted to understand the relationship between Him and His Father in several different and often amusing ways, in the hope of avoiding any misunderstandings that might lead to tri-theism (belief in three separate gods). The Monarchists were unsuccessful in the long run, nevertheless, the idea of restricting the humanity of Christ continued, unabated, in the East. Some heresies completely denied His humanity.

Docetism (**Dokesis**) is derived from the Greek word meaning "semblance," or "appearance" (44). The Docetists believed that Jesus, the biological Christ, was man in appearance only and that He only appeared to suffer and to die on the cross. In this way, the Docetists avoided the "degrading" or "humiliating" death of the Messiah, as a divine person. Thus, the Docetists, also called the "Seemists," proclaimed the body of Christ to be an "optical illusion," a form of "phantomism" and hence, they denied His humanity, totally (45); for them, Jesus was a pure spirit.

From pure spirit it was a simple step to Gnosticism. The term, Gnosis, means knowledge, not rational knowledge, but a hidden, mystical, knowledge obtained from prayer and reflection upon the Scriptures. (The Gnostic movement in the second century A.D. may be traced back to Simon Magus of Gitta, in Samaria; its thesis was propagated by Maricon, Basilides, and Valentinus.)

Gnostic knowledge is obtained by "participation" in the divine mystery, to grant its followers spiritual "union" with God and, consequently, "salvation." It goes beyond "simple faith" and "reason" to avoid all reality and , thus, it was in effect, another side of Docetism (46).

28

Gnosticism as a doctrine died out but it left a relative behind that the church could live with; monasticism (47). About 250 A.D., Egyptian Christians fleeing persecution established an ascetic way of life in the depths of the desert. They rejected the worldiness about them in favor of what has been called "the hermit ideal"; and they set about physical and intellectual labor to honor Christ and to help the needy. Many of them were non-Hellenized Copts and thereby avoided the usual brands of heresy.

The last major heresy to upset the early church was Arianism (48). In 321 A.D., Arius was appointed to the priesthood in Alexandria, and he came under the influence of Origen's writings. For Arius, only God (the Father) is "eternal" and "unoriginated" and, consequently, Jesus could not be co-eternal with Him, for there was a time when Jesus (the biological Christ) did not exist on Earth (prior to His birth). Therefore, Jesus is not fully God or man to Arius but, perhaps, something in between. Athanasius, Bishop of Alexandria (328-373 A.D.), vehemently opposed the doctrine of Arius by calling for a church council at Nicaea to meet in May of 325 A.D., to discuss the issue. The church leaders upheld the doctrine that Jesus is of one substance **(homoousios)** with the Father and in no way inferior to Him. While the biological Christ was indeed born in time, the spiritual Christ was eternal. Arius was condemned for heresy, but his thoughts lived on in the East, in somewhat modified form.

The Nicaean Council also established a new precedent. Since the third century, the bishops of Rome, Alexandria and Antioch, three major Holy Sees, were accorded great prestige and honor, and their authority extended well beyond those cities. By the fifth century, the church recognized that reality, and, in a new attempt to consolidate authority over the other bishops and more effectively fight local heresies, the office of Patriarch was developed and approved (49). A Patriarchate for Jerusalem was created as well, but the most prestigious Patriarchate in the East remained at Constantinople, the seat of the Byzantine Empire. The patriarchs became the heads of several national churches and rites within the Catholic (Universal) Church.

This development, the reconstitution of the Holy Sees, did not, however, end the theological disputes. One last and major struggle had to be waged.

Nestorius, a Cilician educated at Antioch, became Patriarch of Constantinople (428-431 A.D.) and taught that the divine and human natures of Christ were in absolute harmony, but not in one person (50). Antioch opposed this view and Nestorius was condemned at the Council of Ephesus, in 431 A.D. His concepts underwent modification and effected the rise of Monophysitism.

Syria became the stronghold of the Monophysite heresy. Basically, that movement maintained that Jesus possessed only one nature, the divine one, with His human nature subordinated to practical non-existence. The term "mono-physite" means "one nature," in this case the divine one. The antecedent of this heresy can be traced back to Apollinaris of Laodicea, in Syria, and, hence, it had a natural base of operation there. His followers denied the complete humanity of Jesus emphasizing His divinity (51). The Council of Chalcedon (451 A.D.) condemned both the Nestorian and Monophysite doctrines. After completing its investigations, the council proclaimed the two perfect and separate natures of Christ as "orthodox" Christian belief; it is still considered so by the Catholic, the Orthodox and the Protestant churches.

In a final attempt to bring the un-orthodox Christians back to mainstream Christianity, a new doctrine was considered in the seventh century to try to bridge the gap between the remaining Monophysites and the Universal Church. The new Monothelite creed was a compromise, accepting two separate natures for Christ, but only one divine will (52). This doctrine was ingenious but unsuccessful. It was condemned by both the Lateran Council of Rome in 649 A.D. and by the sixth ecumenical council of Constantinople in 680-681 A.D. Although it died a double death, it was revived again.

In the Near East, the Syriac using church split into two groups, the Eastern Syrian Church which was an off-shoot of Nestorianism, and the Western Syrian Church which retained a Monophysite base (53). In the sixth century, the West Syrian Church was also known as the Jacobite Church, named after Jacob Baradaeus, Bishop of Edessa (approximately 543 A.D.). The Jacobite Church was also called the Old Syrian Church.

Many of the remaining churches in the Near East remained faithful to the councils of Nicaea and Chalcedon, such as the

Melkite (royal or kings) Church which became part of the Byzantine Orthodox Church, and the Maronite Church of Lebanon which maintained its independence from Byzantium and upheld its theoretical purity to later become a part of the Eastern Rite Catholic Churches (54). (They were once charged with accepting Monohpysite or Monothelite tenents, but those accusations have been firmly refuted (55).

The Maronite Church (56) traces its origins to Saint Maron (Mar Maroun) an ascetic monk who founded a "monastery" in the fourth century A.D. (d. 410 A.D.). He established the pious foundations of the church in the Syrian wilderness near Antioch. His disciples relocated to Qal'at al-Madiq, on the Orontes River and built a monastery in his memory. There, they ran afoul of the Jacobits and many of them suffereed martyrdom. Later, they moved into the mountains of Lebanon where they effectively defended themselves and spread their faith. Yuhanna Maroun became one of their most noted bishops and the first patriarch of their church, taking the title Patriarch of Antioch And All The East. He began to mold a militarily powerful, intellectually brilliant, and culturally high civilization from among the natives of Lebanon; in time, that Christian community fought defensively against both the armies of Byzantium and the mighty surge of Islam, to retain independence and freedom of religion. But it is Saint Maron, however, who is credited with founding a church and a nation from among the indigenous dwellers of the Lebanon.

The task attained, the commission realized, the church survived its own heresies and expanded into the far flung corners of the world. Some scholars see its success, against all forms of adversity, as a result of the genius of a few individuals, or the faith and martyrdom of many; some see it as a result of the legalization of Christianity by Galerius (311 A.D.) and Constantine (313 A.D.); some see it as an intellectual success spanning the gap between Hebrew philosophy, Hellenic thought, and Roman legalism; some see it as a result of the legislative prerogatives of the Christian Church; and, lastly, some attribute it to the end of the era of out-dated paganism, worn-out mythologies, and worthless atheism, or to the beginning of a new age of belief. All those theories have had a place in the preceeding pages, but something more is needed. The early Christians believed that the Holy spirit, at work in their lives, would lead them and the Universal Church to victory

31

against bitter persecution and tremendous odds. The church could be hurt, but it would never die, for Christ had already "cheated" death, taking away its power. And, now for one last observation; perhaps the time was right, the right time (**kairos**) had come for God to directly intervene in human affairs, so that His church and doctrines would come to fruition in this world. Had the world failed in its mission, that is, succumbed to the pagan world about it, then the life and teachings of Jesus of Nazareth would have been forgotten, or consigned to a footnote of history. It may just be that the hand of God was the true force that enabled the commission to be fulfilled.

CHAPTER TWO NOTES

1. Charles Guignebert, **The Early History of Christianity,** N.Y.: Twayne Pub., 1927. p.51.

2. Eusebius, **The History of The Church,** N.Y.: Penguin Books, 1981, pp. 99-102; Henry Chadwick, **The Early Church,** N.Y.: Penguin Books, 1983, p. 18.

3. Raymond Brown, **The Churches the Apostles Left Behind,** N.Y.: Paulist Press, 1984, pp. 14-15.

4. Chadwick **op. cit.,** p. 17.

5. Peters, **op. cit.,** pp. 488, 491. For a full discussion of the Jerusalem church see: Peters, **op. cit.,** pp. 487-492.

"History records the names of several men who founded religions, others who fathered nations, still others who instituted states; but if there ever was a man, other than Muhammad, who initiated all three institutions, history must have forgotten his name. The three founded by Muhammad were originally extricably interwoven and to an extent interdependent. Throughout their careers the first-religion provided the integrating force and proved to be the most enduring."

Philip K. Hitti
Makers of Arab History

6. **Ibid.,** p. 488.

7. Chadwick, **op. cit.,** pp. 16-17.

8. Peters, **op. cit.,** p. 494.

9. **Ibid.** p. 496.

10. **Ibid.,** p. 489; For the later history of Antioch see: Sweetman, **op. cit.,** part 1, vol. I, pp. 49-50.

11. Chadwick, **op. cit.,** p. 9.

12. The following description of the evolutionary agent of the logos is taken from: Tillich, **op. cit.,** pp. 7-8, 11-15, 28-29; Peters, **op. cit.,** pp. 134-136, 304-305.

13. See: Kee, **op. cit.,** p. 244-245; Tillich, **op. cit.,** pp. 29-32; Peters, **op. cit.,** p. 499.

14. Eusebius, **op. cit.,** pp. 132-133. Many of Christianity's supporters of detractors, of all faiths as well as the lack of faith, believe that the application of reason (logic) - the logos - to Christian doctrine has made it the most logical religion in the world. Consequently, that process continued into the Middle Ages as a form of Scholasticism and, today, it is still manifest in Christian theology and Christology.

15. An Apostalic See is a seat of a bishop were priests could be ordained, disputes could be settled and church councils could be held. The first See is Jerusalem, followed by Antioch, Constantinople (now Istanbul), Rome and Alexandria. This study is primarily concerned with the See of Antioch and the East. Eusebius, **op. cit.,** p. 11; Raymond E. Brown and John P. Meier, **Antioch and Rome,** N.Y.: Paulist Press, 1983, pp. 66-67.

16. Eusebius, **op. cit.,** p. 18; Peters, **op. cit.,** p. 491.

17. On the early structure of the church see: Peters, **op. cit.,** pp. 491-492; Chadwick, **op. cit.,** p. 46; Brown and Meier, **Antioch...,** p. 13; Brown, **The Churches...,** pp. 17, 32-33.

18. For a full discussion of the significance of these issues see: Brown and Meier, **op. cit.,** pp. 2-8, 41-43.

19. **Ibid.,** pp. 2-8.

20. **Ibid.,** pp. 41-43; Peters, **op. cit.,** p. 493; Chadwick, **op. cit.,** pp. 19-20.

21. Chadwick, **op. cit.,** pp. 22-23; Peters, **op. cit.,** p. 491.

22. Chadwick, **op. cit.,** pp 22-23.

23. **Ibid.,** p. 21; Brown and Meier, **op. cit.,** p. 49; Peters, **op. cit.,** p. 490.

24. Brown's classification, **op. cit.,** p. 15.

25. Eusebius, **op. cit.,** p. 23; Brown, **op. cit.,** p. 24.

26. Brown, **op. cit.,** p. 24; Peters, **op. cit.,** p. 492.

27. Eusebius, **op. cit.,** pp. 97-98.

28. Peters, **op. cit.,** pp. 483-484.

29. **Ibid.,** p. 500; Brown and Meier, **op. cit.,** pp. 13, 15, 24, 51.

30. Brown and Meier, **op. cit.,** pp. 57-59, 62; Peters, **op. cit.,** p. 500.

31. Eusebius, **op. cit.,** pp. 134-135; Kee, **op. cit.,** pp. 261-269; Peters, **op. cit.,** pp. 505-506.

32. On the Gnostic Gospels see: Elaine Pagels, **The Gnostic Gospels,** N.Y.: Vintage Books, 1981; Kee, **op. cit.,** pp. 269-280; Peters, **op. cit.,** pp. 653-654.

33. Chadwick, **op. cit.,** pp. 43-44.

34. Peters, **op. cit.,** pp. 502-504.

35. Chadwick, **op. cit.,** pp. 38-41; Kee, **op. cit.,** pp. 259, 280-281; Tillich, **op. cit.,** p. 34.

36. On this church see: Aziz S. Atiya, **History of Eastern Christianity,** Indiana: University of Notre Dame Press, 1968.

37. On this movement see: Chadwick, **op. cit.**, pp. 221-222.

38. **Ibid.** p. 221.

39. The exact forms of the Sacraments and their place in the Mass and elsewhere were not standardized until the early Middle Ages in the West. During the Reformation, they became part of the controversy over corruption in the Latin (Roman Catholic) Church. Today, thanks to more objective scholarship and an ecumenical spirit, the issue of corruption has been greatly minimized. It is generally accepted that no church can escape corruption and that the accusations against the Roman Catholic Church were greatly exaggerated by writers trying to make a point, in the absence of reliable statistics or data.

The main issue in the Reformation was the unresolvable clash between the doctrines of free will and predestination which had plagued Jewish scholars and, later, Islamic theology. Predestination could make the need for Sacraments unnecessary while free will could make them mandatory. (The theory of predestination may be traced back to the philosophy of Augustine, Bishop of Hippo, 395-430 A.D.)

40. Peters, **op. cit.**, p. 492.

41. Chadwick, **op. cit.**, pp. 52, 89; Tillich, **op. cit.**, pp. 40-41; Peters, **op. cit.**, pp. 629-630.

42. On him and his doctrine see: Peters, **op. cit.**, p. 630; Tillich, **op. cit.**, pp. 65-66; Chadwick, **op. cit.**, p. 114.

43. Reconstructed from Chadwick, **op. cit.**, pp. 85-90, 115; Tillich, **op. cit.**, pp. 64-67; Peters, **op. cit.**, 690-691; Sweetman, **op. cit.**, vol. 1, part 1, p. 60.

44. Guigneberg, **op. cit.**, pp. 145-147; Chadwick, **op. cit.**, pp. 37-38.

45. Kee, **op. cit.**, p. 259; Chadwick, **op. cit.**, p. 37.

46. On this construction see: Peters, **op. cit.**, pp. 648-662; Tillich, **op. cit.**, pp. 33-37; Chadwick, **op. cit.**, p. 35.

47. Chadwick, **op. cit.**, pp. 174-178; Tillich, **op. cit.**, p. 145; Peters, **op. cit.**, pp. 639-643.

48. On this movement see: Peters, **op. cit.**, pp. 689-692; Tillich, **op. cit.**,pp. 69-72; Chadwick, **op. cit.**, pp. 130-136; Sweetman, **op. cit.**, vol. 1, part 1, p. 59.

49. Chadwick, **op. cit.**, pp. 51, 131.

50. **Ibid.**, pp. 194-200; P. K. Hitti, **The Near East in History,** N.Y.: Van Nostrand, 1961, p. 161; On Antioch see: Sweetman, **op. cit.**, vol. 1, part 1, pp. 49-50.

51. Chadwick, **op. cit.**, pp. 148, 200-212.

52. **Ibid.**, p. 210.

53. Hitti, **op. cit.**, pp. 176-177.

54. The Eastern Rite consists of two main groups, those of the Byzantine or Syriac litergy and the Malabar Rite. All of them are completely Catholic and recognize the Pope of Rome. On the Maronite Church or Rite see: **The New Catholic Ency.**, Vol IX, pp. 245-253.

55. Rev. Pierre Dib, **History of The Maronite Church,** Wash., D.C., chapters two and three; P. K. Hitti, **Lebanon in History,** N.Y.: Macmillan, 1967, p. 251; Atiya, **op. cit.**, part IV, pp. 389-423.

56. Hitti, **Lebanon ...**, pp. 247-249.

CHAPTER THREE

THE LAST MESSENGER

In the sixth century A.D., the Semetic High God, El/Elohim (Yahweh), who had made a covenant with Abraham, who had given His Commandments to Moses, that same God (Elah) whom Jesus had called Abba,His Father in Heaven, and He who called Jesus His Beloved Son, that self-same Lord of the Universe, al-Ilah (Allah), decided, once again, to reveal His will and laws to mankind. This time the recipient of His message was to an Arabian, Muhammad, the son of Aminah and Abd Allah (of the Hashimite clan of the Quraysh tribe), known to his companians and friends as al-Amin, the trustworthy.

The life of the Prophet Muhammad was first recorded by Muhammad Ibn Ishaq (d. 767 A.D.) but his study is no longer in existence. The task then fell to Ibn Hisham (d. 833 A.D.) and his work remains the basic text for all biographies of the Prophet of Islam (1). Although compiled almost two centuries after Muhammad's death, it is still considered the standard text on his life. Rigorous efforts were made to verify the biography's contents from other sources, but some early Islamic scholars believed that the accounts were embellished with lore, legend, and miracle stories that may not be verifiable; nevertheless, there is nothing in the biography of the prophet to indicate any actions or words that could discredit his claim to prophethood, or that were contrary to it.

There are, for example, stories (2) that the prophet's mother never felt any ill effects of her pregnancy and was not aware of her condition until she was told of it by an angel of the Lord; others say the prophet's wet nurse, long dry at the time, felt her breasts fill with milk upon setting her gaze upon him; still others relate the tale that when the infant prophet grew ill, angels extracted a blood clot or, perhaps, a gall stone, from his chest to relieve the pressure. All those accounts circulated for the first time long after Muhammad's death with, possibly, the exception of the last one which may be Quranic in origin.

38

Most scholars of Islam agree that the prophet's only miracle is the inimitability (**i'jaz**) of the Quran, Islam's Holy Book. But, others cite miracles (3) as signs associated with his mission such as the splitting of the moon; the crying of a branch or stem of a date palm tree; the flowing of water from in between the fingers of the prophet; a greeting by the stones of the streets of Mecca as the prophet passed near them; the inability to bury the body of a Christian renegade from Islam; the trees that bowed to shade and cover the prophet for modesty's sake; the drawing of water from the long dried well of Hudaibiyah; an increased date harvest in response to the prophet's prayers; a wolf that spoke in praise of God's apostle and, lastly, the prophet's night journey to paradise. Most of those narratives were collected from the prophet's companions through a very long line of transmitters, several centuries after the original communicant's death. They remain, therefore, to this day a matter of individual belief or disbelief, among Moslem scholars. There is, however, much that is factual in the Prophet Muhammad's biography.

Muhammad was born in Mecca in 570 A.D., into an Arabia that was pagan in heart and soul. Nearly every form of immorality was available for the right price. The Arabians refer to this period as the "age of ignorance," al-jahiliyah (4), to denote ignorance of the one true God and His moral and ethical laws and decrees. It was an age of superstition and blood-feuds, of infanticide and raids, of opulent wealth and miserable poverty. All along the western coast of Arabia, where the caravan trade flourished, were temples of prostitution where momentary pleasures could be negotiated. The center of Arabian life was the sophisticated city of Mecca where the Quraysh tribe controlled the city's abundant wealth, the center of religious life and pilgramage, and the Ka'bah (a cube structured sanctuary) which housed many religious fetishes and a curious Black Stone.

The pagan religions of Arabia consisted of many forms from local tribal dieties to complex Grecco-Roman dynastic gods, to Hindu tritheism, to astrial triads, but in general, the religious atmosphere was extremely tolerant. The chief diety of the Arabians was Allah (the God) aided by his daughters al-Lat, al-Uzza and Manat (5). Among the pagans there also lived several Christian communities, some Jews in the city of Yathrib and in southern Arabia, and a strange indigenous group of monotheists belonging to neither Christianity or Judaism, but influenced by both of them, known as the Hanifs. One of the best known Hanifs was Waraqah ibn Nawfal who became a Christian and translated part of the Gospels into Arabic. (He was related to the Prophet Muhammad through marriage.)

Of Muhammad's birth and early life not much is known. His father, Abd Allah, died before he was born and his mother, Aminah, passed away when he was six years old. He first lived as an orphan with his grandfather, Abd al-Muttalib, until he died and then with his uncle, Abu-Talib. For the next seventeen years, practically nothing about Muhammad is known. Almost all sources are silent but others hint at his interest in and, perhaps attachment to, the Hanif community - its monotheistic ideas may have impacted upon him.

At the age of twenty-five, we find the future prophet (**nabi**) and messaner (**rasul**) of God at work for a wealthy widow named Khadijah. He was employed in her long distance caravan trade and, later, he married her, although she was some fifteen years older than him. While on a business venture to Syria, legend states that Muhammad met a Christian monk named Bahira who recognized the light and sigh of prophethood in the young man. it is quite possible that either the Hanifs, Bahira, or both of them were agents of the Lord, acting as a herald for Muhammad, just as John the Baptist had been for the coming of Christ.

As a young man, Muhammad shunned the various forms of immoral pleasures available to him in the city of Mecca, perferring to meditate in the cool solitude of the caves outside the city. There, in those quiet confines, he pondered the world he lived in, and particularly why his people were left in ignorance of God, without a Book to guide the, similar to the Holy Books of the Christians and Jews. He must have felt that his people were morally lost and adrift, like a powerless ship on an open sea, in their pleasure-bent society. Then, the Night of Power descended upon him!

On that night, in 610 A.D., while Muhammad was deep in contemplation, he heard a voice, later identified as the angel Gabriel, commanding the semi-literate man to read and recite in the name of the Lord:

Recite, in the name of thy Lord,
who created,
Created man from a clot of blood (meaning the embryo)

Furthermore:

Read for thy Lord is most bounteous,
Who teacheth by the pen,
Teacheth man what he did not know.

The message was later accompanied by a resounding reverberation of bells. The first call, on that night, had summoned Muhammad to the service of the Semetic High God, the one and only true God of all mankind, the Lord of the Worlds.

Filled with fear and trepidation, he did not fully understand why he, an unaccomplished speaker or writer when compared to the great literary poets of Arabia, should bear an enormous responsibility for his people. He went home and told his wife of the vision and voice in the cave, and then wrapped himself in blankets, as if to hide. But the angel of the Lord was relentless; Muhammad, now in a trance-like state, heard the voice again, saying:

O' thou, enwrapped in thy mantle,
Arise and warn.

The process complete, now fully a prophet for his people, Muhammad would arise and warn them of the consequences of their behavior, in a continuing message that would only cease with his death, in 632 A.D.

The task was not easy. The Meccans saw his message as a major threat to both their beliefs and livelihood. (They opposed him from the beginning of his mission.) The more he preached about the oneness of God, and a moral preception of life, the more dangerous Mecca became for him.

He won a few converts at first. Among them were his wife, Khadijah, and his cousin, Ali, who later became his son-in-law. He attrached the lower classes and a few followers from the lower middle class, those who sought a better life that was beyond their reach. As his following grew in numbers, his clan,

41

the Hashimites, were hard pressed to cease protecting him. They refused, but the prophet saw it prudent to sent some of his supporters to the Christian kingdom of Abyssinia, for protection.

At Mecca, Abu Talib continued to protect Muhammad out of clan loyalty, even though he never believed in his prophethood (6). With the death of Abu Talib and Khadijih, the prophet's position in Mecca became extremely precarious.

Muhammad was being accused of possession by the jinn (genie/an evil spirit or being), of magic or sorcery, and of being nothing more than a soothsayer; on a trip to Taif to preach, he was ridiculed, insulted and stoned. After that incident, the prophet decided to leave Mecca for Yathrib, to the north, where his presence was sought as an intercessor and arbitrator among the communities seeking to order a society in flux. Muhammad escaped from Mecca to Yathrib now called the city of the prophet (Madinat al-Nabi) or simply Medina, in September of 622. (The Moslem calendar begins with that year, the Hijrah (his migration).

From Medina, the prophet went on the offensive against the enemies of God. Legislation from the Lord provided for the struggle (jihad). Clearly, Muhammad became a prophet in the warrior-prophet tradition of the Old Testament. Also, from the pre-Hijrah period falls the prophet's noctural journey from the Ka'bah via Jerusalem to the seventh heaven (his mi'raj). The details of this miraculous journey made Jerusalem sacred to Moslems, and provided the believer with details of a paradise that awaits the fallen martyr (7). Some Moslems believe the sojourn to have been a dream-like state; while others insist upon its physical reality. The pagans, of course, accused Muhammad of having hallucinated but, nevertheless, he did confirm a view of paradise, and the benefits of fighting in the path of God for his followers. Soon afterward, Muhammad's men began harrassing the Meccan caravans.

In Medina, the prophet won new converts from the city (the Ansar) and he began to rely on them, for he won no support form among the city's Jewish inhabitants. At first, the Jews welcomed him but, later, rejected him and his mission, for Muhammad insisted that Jesus was the expected Messiah, and that he was the last prophet in the Abrahamic line, even though Muhammad was not well versed in the Jewish Scriptures.

42

As Muhammad's ranks swelled, the Meccans decided to end his constant annoying interference with their trade. The wells of Badr were to be the scene of a climatic battle between the opposing sides. Muhammad commanded about 314 men facing an army of approximately 900 troops of the Quraysh. Without a battle plan and somewhat over confident, the Meccans were completed defeated, put to flight, leaving the field of combat in complete disarray. Their booty fell to the Moslems, under God's sanction. But, the Meccans regrouped for another attempt near a hill named Uhud.

This time, in March of 625, the Meccans prepared an elaborate battle plan. Led by Abu Sufyan, they attacked the prophet and his followers, but, with the aid and intercession of angels, the prophet's men held the hill, although Muhammad was wounded several times. The limited success of the Meccans encouraged them to try harder.

The siege of Medina was a follow up campaign to the battle of Uhud, intended to besiege the city and force it to surrender or capitulate. The city was protected by trenches, a tactic accredited to a Persian convert and, thus, the ten thousand man Meccan army was unable to breach its defenses for more than three months. Consequently, they withdrew from the field of battle, once again lacking a victory.

After three unsuccessful attempts against the Prophet Muhammad, the Meccans decided to accept his leadership. For the Moslems, the victories were seen as the fulfillment of God's will. (Only one strong opponent remained, the Jews of Khaybar. They were reduced by combat and made to pay a tribute.)

Victory now complete, the prophet made his peace with his former enemies in the Treaty of Hudaybiyah (named after a location 9 miles north of Mecca), in 628 A.D., on the basis of Islam as a sort of state religion. Muhammad's political leadership was also fully recogized at that time. It is believed that in this period the prophet sent letters to the rulers of Egypt, Byzantium and Persia requesting their conversion to Islam.

Two years later the prophet entered Mecca thriumphantly; he entered the Ka'bah and smashed the idols saying, "Truth hath come, and falsehood had vanished (8)." Only the Black Stone, associated with Judaism, remained within its walls. The sanctuary was purified and dedicated to Allah. Muhammad's former enemies were treated magnanimously. And the prophet rode at the head of a delegation from each of the seven major clans, circumambulating (**tawaf**) the Ka'bah, to demonstrate the equality of all Arabian tribes.

In the following years, Muhammad received duputations from all over Arabia submitting to his God and to the new religion called Islam (submission). He made plans for further conquests, but soon after Muhammad grew ill, complaining of headaches. He died on June 8, 632, in the city of Medina; he was buried in a simple ceremony under the floor of the mud hut of his favorite wife, A'ishah. Muhammad's life ended as simply as it had begun; he sought nothing material from this world, only the truth motivated him, and that is precisely what he left for his followers.

Muhammad wrote down nothing of this revelations. That task went to his followers. During his life, Muhammad received the revelations of God through the assistance of the angel Gabriel; and although the prophet spoke the words of the Quran, they are believed to be the Words of God by devout Moslems. As the prophet spoke the holy words, in a trance-like state, they were recorded upon the materials at hand - "palm leaves," "stones," "leather," and in the "hearts of men," that is, those who memorized them (the huffaz).

Shortly after the death of Muhammad, many of the tribes that had pledged their allegiance to him and to Islam reneged upon their word. Thus, the first "major war" in Islam occurred under the direction of Abu Bakr (632-634 A.D.), the political successor (Caliph) of the prophet. The wars of riddah (secession or apostacy) took many lives and established the first civil war of Islam - there is no conversion from Islam. Anyone is free to become a Moslem, but it is illegal for anyone to convert from Islam. (Freedom of religion is, therefore, a one-way street in Islam, enter you may, leave and you will suffer extinction.) In 633 A.D., another major campaign was launched against a false prophet, Musaylima, thus ending the lives of many more of the caliph's men who had memorized the Quran.

On the advice of Umar ibn al-Khattab, Abu Bakr approached Muhammad's secretary, Zayd ibn Thabit of Medina, to collect the available revelations into a single volume before too many of the memorizers were killed in battle and and serious gaps in the text could occur. The project took approximately five years to complete (657 A.D.), and it was plagued with many problems.

The earthly Quran (recitation/reading) was first compiled in segments which separated the Meccan chapters (suras) from those revealed in Medina. They were then combined into a complete text, and the Medina codex was "canonized."

During the Caliphate of Uthman (644-656 A.D.), Umar's successor, various readings of the Quran had developed and, consequently, the caliph appointed Zayd to a committee to revise the Quran. Umar's copy, kept with his daughter Hafsah who was also one of Muhammad's widows, became the basic reference. The new, "revised," edition became the standard text (9). All other copies were destroyed, and the new text was duplicated and dispatched to the Arabian encampments in Damascus, al-Basrah, and al-Kufah.

Some modern scholars maintain that Uthman canonized the Medina codex because it was in the prophet's dialect (Qurayshi) and destroyed the others because he had tampered with the original text. (This was the charge made by some of the supporters of Ali for the caliphate against Uthman.) Others say that the varying copies were destroyed to prevent more than one Quran from existing with contradictions or different readings or varying emphasis and interpretations, charges that were later aimed at the four Gospels of Christianity. All this is, however, academic speculation. And, indeed, it did not prevent the generation of apocryphal Qurans at a later time. The final text of the Quran was completed in 933 A.D., almost three centuries after the death of Prophet Muhammad, when the proper diacritical marks and vowels were added to its corpus.

Translations of the Quran into foreign languages are a recent phenomenon; the Quran was revealed in Arabic, believed by the Arabians to be the language of God, for the Arabian community near Mecca. As the Arabians began to conquer non-Arabic speaking peoples and to impose their faith upon them, they taught some of those peoples their language. Today, however, it is impractical to expect all Moslems to learn Arabic, hence, the Quran has been translated into many tongues under titles that imply something less than an accurate, perfect copy, for that, after all, is a theologically impossible task. The Quran is inimitable in its Arabic form, structure and words.

There are, nevertheless, excellent translations of that Scripture, such as Yusuf Ali's **The Holy Qur-An** with explanatory notes to give the current Moslen interpretation of the text. Others like Mohammed Marmaduke Pickthall's **The Meaning of the Glorious Koran,** written by a convert to Islam, betray some extremely serious errors in, perhaps, an effort to win new converts to the faith, or to give a clearer meaning to a verse (as the title indicates) which may be lacking in the desired precision or understanding, or to change its intent. (Compare, for example, the text of verse 4: 171 in Pickthall's translation and in Ali's translation where they have added the words "only" and "no more than" to the English text regarding the role of Jesus as a prophet. Those worlds are missing in the original Arabic text. This is done to give the English reader the positive impression that God, and not the translator or interpreter has limited the role of Jesus to only that of a prophet, messenger, or Apostle, and therfore, one might come to the conclusion that Jesus is certainly not the Son of God or the Lord. More on Quranic exegesis **(tafsir)** will be given in another chapter.)

The structure and words of the Arabic Quran are unique. There was no prototype text or analogous book to follow. The earthly Quran is believed to be identical to a copy preserved in the seventh heaven, near the throne of God, called the "Mother Book," or the "The Guarded Tablet." The Quran is, therefore, uncreated; it is eternal! The book consists of 114 chapters, ninety of which were revealed at Mecca and deal with the oneness of God, His attributes, heaven and hell, the final judgment, and the duties of man; the remaining chapters revealed at Medina are more administrative and legislative concerning war, punishments for crime, civil rights, and political, economic, social and cultural life.

But Islam is much more than the above notions and, clearly, its message is far deper, in both content and intention. The Quran stresses the oneness of God **(tawhid)** (10). It opposes polytheism, pantheism, atheism, or the belief in any god or gods other than Allah. No partners, human or divine, can be associated with God. The Quran points to biological creation as evidence of God's existence; He sent messengers to mankind to guide them, for the human race is not a free and frivolous creature. "The religion of/with God is Islam," and , thus, the culture of God is Islamic. That means that all cultures, ideologies, and religions are at best only semi-valid, or they are totally invalid. The semi-valid faiths/ ideologies are Judaism, Christianity and Zoroastrianism (mentioned in the Quran). All else is unacceptable in the eyes of God and the true believer. The first message of the Quran, therefore, is that "there is no God but Allah"; and that Islam is for all mankind, whether one wants it or not.

Prophethood is the major instrument of God. The prophet is the tie-in to revelation (11); the link between the two is faith. Muhammad came in the prophetic tradition of the Old and New Testament. However, he is also "the Seal of the Prophets" - originally a Persian title, but now given new meaning. Muhammad is the last in a long line of prophets, therefore, he excels all others because he has brought to fruition the last message of the Semetic High God. He is the perfect guide for human kind, he has completed and perfected God's message, forever. That Muhammad is the messenger of God, with the final and consummate revelation, is the second message of the Quran. The proof of Muhammad's mission was his success, and that his coming was foretold in both the Torah and the Gospels, according to the Moslem scholars who sought to identify Muhammad with words or phrases in the older revealed texts (12).

The problem of good and evil is dealt with as a major theme in the Quran (13). The Quran exhorts man to "do good" and "avoid evil," and it promises paradise for the beliver and the fiery garden of hell for the non-believers. Piety (14) is the measure of compliance since all Moslemss, good or bad, go to paradise. But, punishment awaits evil doers on Earth and the Day of Judgment awaits them in heaven.

In Islam, there are two major categories of sin against God. The greatest sin against God is the unpardonable act of ascribing partners to God (shirk) or ascribing divine authority, attributes or power to someone or something other than God. Partnership with God may take many forms including major and minor acts to even inconspicuous events, such as ingratitute towards God. Disbelief (**kufr**) is also classified in terms of major and minor sins such as denial of divine truth or excessive pride to doubting one's own convictions, or hypocrisy.

And, lastly, Islam strives for an ethical and moral code of life for all Moslems, and a world view that encourages justice. To that extent, it has its own "commandments (15)."

1. "Belief in one God

2. Honoring one's mother and father

3. Respecting the rights of others

4. Being generous an considerate of kin ties

5. Avoiding unjustifiable killing

6. Do not commit adultery

7. Safeguarding the possessions of orphans; treating orphans kindly

8. Deal justly and equitable with neighbors

9. Be pure of heart and mind and give truthful testimony

10. Be humble and unpretentious."

To achieve and accomplish the above, highly desired results, certain mechanisms came into being, the most important of which was Islamic Law (the Shari'ah/the path) which will be discussed in more detail in another chapter.

Added to the belief-system (Iman) - Unity of God, Prophethood of Muhammad, the Uncreated Quran, the angels and jinn, and the final day of judgment - are the articles of faith (Ibadat/"acts of Devotion") which have become the pillars of Islam (Arkan al-Din), approximately equivalent to the Sacraments in Christianity. They are:

1. To bear witness (the Shahadah) that there exists only one God, and that Muhammad is His messenger. This is the fundamental creed of Islam and its basic dogma. To profess this is to be a Moslem.

2. Prayer (Salat) is required five times a day - morning, noon, midday, sunset and at night. The prayer must be in Arabic and one must face Mecca; proper cleanliness is also necessary.

3. Alms giving (Zakah) became a tax on Moslems for the benefit of the Moslem community (ummah), now to be separated and above all others.

4. Fasting (Sawm) occurs during the month of Ramadan, from sunrise to sunset, as a form of penance, and to identify with the fate of poor Moslems.

5. Pilgramage (Hajj) to Mecca should be made at least once in a lifetime if possible. At Mecca, the pilgrim circumambulates the Ka'bah, as Muhammad did, representing the conquest of Islam over paganism.

6. Struggle (Jihad) in the path of God, also called Holy War, is sometimes considered a pillar of the faith, due to its significance, for the fallen martyr goes immediately to Paradise.

Islam divides the world into two great, yet opposing, spheres of influence, the Moslem Worldd (Dar al-Islam) and the non-Moslem World (Dar al-Harb/the abode of war). To achieve the Islamification of this world, which belongs to God, its creator, and to whom all allegiance and sovereignty is due, a Moslem may struggle against the non-Moslems, by exertions (jihad) in the name of God. This can be done by open warfare, by the pen, by word, or by self-purification (example), in order to win new converts to the faith. Islamic law, however, became the most potent of the peaceful methods aimed at converting the nonbeliever.

Although definitely not a pillar of Islam, the veiling of women has assumed the importance of a pillar of faith in some Islamic societies. The veiling and seclusion of women is an ancient Near Eastern custom elaborated by the Assyrians (1500-1200

B.C.) and the Medes; it is not particulary a Christian or Moslem institution. But, both those religions called for modesty in dress in the presence of pagans.

It must be recalled that Islam, like Judaism, was revealed in a pagan society where lust and contract regulated the male-female sexual relationship. And, pagan Arabia ascribed to the ancient view that the human body was inciteful and immoral. Therefore, in order for Moslem women to protect themselves from the lecherous gaze of pagan men, the veiling of women and their segregation from the mainstream of society came about. In time, the segregated roles reinforced the social system but they also produced negative sexual hypertension resulting in their continued need. Thus, the Islamic dress code for women came into existence as a device to protect women, but it is often misunderstood in the West where a different attitude towards human sexuality evolved.

Christianity entered a Hebrew culture where a strong sense of morality already existed and, thereafter, the male-female relationship took on a sacramental nature, rooted in love, not lust.

In Islam, the call for veiled women still exists to protect Moslem women from Moslem men who may be less noble than desired, from "the temptation of males," and to prevent women from becoming "sex objects," or a "turn-on."

In the modern world where equality between men and women exist, those precautions have become meaningless for the role of women has expanded in society, consequently, women are no longer only sexual receptacles for the male. (In the West, similar attitudes toward women survive in unassimilable sub-cultures.) More importantly, from a Christian perspective, the veiling and seclusion of women violates the absolute justice of God by making Him prejudice against women or in favor of men.

Since Muhammad is Islam's greatest personality, his example is to be followed. His style of life should be emulated and his teachings (**Hadith**/speech) adhered to at all times. The unwritten customs (**Sunnah**) of the prophet were studied and, Arabian culture was purified so that sixth century Arabia became the Islamic cultural "ideal," for all times and places. Indeed, God would never let His community agree on an error. The traditions of the prophet, written (**Hadith**) or unwritten (**Sunnah**), became all important, as a source for Islam and to cover incidents not referred to in the Quran.

Shortly after the prophet's demise, the search for his legitimate sayings began, as a source of undisputed authority (16). It began in the city of Medina, among the pious and, soon after, the process became a science unto itself. As time passed, in the span of two and one-half centuries, more than 600,000 sayings were attributed to Muhammad. The process of collecting them, verifying the truth of each of them, and classifying them became a monumental undertaking. Every Hadith consists of two parts, the chain (**isnad**) of authorities leading back to the first person, and the text (**matn**). The reputation of each person involved was scrutinized and the text was critically analyzed to assure that it would not violate the Quran or the Sunnah. Like the huffaz (memorizers) of the Quran, only the memory of the authorities could not be tested. The best collections were classified as genuine (**sahih**), next came the good/fair ones (**hasan**) and, lastly, weak (**da'if**) sayings. From 600,000 entries, approximately 7,397 sayings were accepted by al-Bukhari, the leading authority on the speech of the prophet. Six canonical collections have been made:

1. **Al-Jami al-Sahih** of Muhammad ibn Isma'il al-Bukhari (d. 870).

2. **Al-Sahih** of Muslim ibm al-Hajjaj (d. 875).

3. **Sunan** of abu Dawud (d. 888).

4. **Jami** of al-Tirmidhi (d. 892).

5. **Sunan** of ibn Majah (d. 886).

6. **Sunan** of al-Nasa'i (d. 915).

The integration of the Quran, the Sunnah, and the Hadith of the prophet became the basis for the day-to-day operation of the Moslem community. (Islamic law will be treated as the cementing force that held the system together, in the next chapter.) The social structure of Islam drew its inspiration from the above works and aimed at a moral and ethical life style and world view (17). In the course of time, its perspectives

51

have been advanced to an extraordinarily high degree that has often been negatively criticized by non-Moslems as "uncivilized," or "barbaric" behavior. Islamic cultural norms are often misunderstood, because non-Moslem societies have evolved with a completely different understanding of similar but basic issues. The amputation of a criminal's arm for theft, the flogging of persons accused of "sexual crimes" (sex outside of marriage), the stoning to death of adulterers, the beating of lesbians and death penalty for homosexuals, the blinding of voyeurs, and the recent trend toward female circumcision to lessen female sexuality (circumcision is required for males only) are not seen as positive aspects of life to encourage morality, in the West. Even the ordering of Islamic society is often found fault with by non-Moslem observers looking at Islam from a different human rights perspective. (An example of the western attitude toward Islamic practices can be found in a recent article in the **Progressive**, August, 1984. It described the case of a young woman who was beaten (whipped) to death for wearing a bathing suit in her own back yard, when a young man saw her and became sexually excited.)

In Islam, an individual's rights are those granted to him or her as part of a group in the Quran. There is no independent concept of human rights for God's decrees superceed all human constructs, always, everywhere and forever. This world has been entrusted by its maker to the Moslem community, to be administered according to God's will, as indicated in the Quran. Islam, therefore, is not just one religion among many; it is for Moslems the only true and valid religion. It places the Moslem man at the top of the social structure with a maximum of rights and prerogatives and, in fact, all Moslem men are equal in God's eyes. Next come Moslem women for "Men are in charge of women, because Allah has made the one of them to excel the other..." The Quran also set forth the following principle, "So good women are the obedient... As for those from whom ye fear rebellion, admonish them and banish them to beds apart, and scourge them." There is neither equality of person or role between Moslem men and women, in the Christian sense. This condition exists to protect women from an immoral, unethical world; and it is believed that women are weaker in faith than men since they commpose the majority in hell, according to a well known Hadith of the Prophet (18). (The achievements of women over men in non-Moslem societies are often seen by deeply religious Moslems as the result of deception or given to them by men in return for sexual favors.)

The non-Moslem peoples fall into two basic categories, those who practice atheism or partnership (**shirk**) with God, and those who are Jews and Christians but are also non-believers (**kafir/kufr**) in the Prophet Muhammad and his mission. For an atheist, polytheist, or pantheist the choice is either conversion or extinction:

> "Then, when the sacred months have passed, slay the idolaters wherever ye find them, and take them captive, and besiege them..."

From the Islamic perspective, nothing is more obnoxious in the sight of God, or a true believer, than one who, for whatever reason, rejects God and His messengers or ascribes partnership to God or worships a false god or gods. It is the only unforgivable sin in Islam (19). And, lastly, for the Jews and Christians who are considered closer to Moslems (more acceptable/preferable) than any non-Moslem community:

> "Fight those who believe not...
>
> Nor acknowledge the Religion

of Truth (even if they are)	(Islam)
of the People of the Book,	(Jews and Christians)
Until they pay the Jizya	(a tax or fine)
With willing submission	(humiliation)
And feel themselves subdued"	(lowly/persecuted)

But, perhaps, the most serious criticism of Islam comes from its acceptance of slavery. The institution of slavery, it should be understood, is almost universal and, therefore, the Moslems were not immune to it. Slavery in the Near East was a natural phenomenon and and intra-racial affair. The ancient Jews could even enslave fellow Jews. Only Christianity totally forbid

53

the practice to their community. The Arabs, Persians and Turks enslaved their own Caucasian race and treated them better than the black slaves taken by other Moslem peoples. When blacks did come under Islamic slavery, however, they were not treated any better by the Moslems than they were by the European Christians (20). Islam does not condemn slavery but it does consider freeing a slave as something pleasing to God. Islamic law regulated the institution to make slavery more humane. Conversion to Islam did not necessarily free a slave, but the children of Moslem slaves were born free, as a divine incentive for conversion.

The above selections from the Quran were chosen to give a general moral tone to western criticism of Islamic doctrines and practices, and to show them, in the light of the foregoing chapter, as a positive force, stressing the basic themes of Islam. For, after all, Islam has ordered society for the well-being of mankind; it is a light in the dark; and it is a path to eternal salvation.

CHAPTER THREE NOTES

1.   For this study I have relied upon Ibn Hisham, **The Biography of The Prophet**, in Arabic, publ. in 2 vol. by Al-Azhar Univ., Cairo, Egypt. For the English translation of this work see: A. Guillaume, **The Life of Muhammad**, Oxford: Oxford Univ. Press, 1978. Shorter academic studies on the life of the Prophet Muhammad include: W. Montgomery Watt, **Muhammad, Prophet and Statesman**, Oxford Univ. Press, 1961; Tor Andre, **Mohammad, The Man and His Faith**, N.Y.: Harper Torchbooks, 1960; Sir John Glubb, **The Life and Times of Muhammad**, N.Y.: Stein and Day, 1971; Sir William Muir, **The Life of Muhammad**, Edinburgh: John Grant, 1912. There are many other excellent biographies of Muhammad in English, many, however, are less academic.

2.   P. K. Hitti, **Makers of Arab History**, N.Y.: Harper Torchbooks, 1968, p. 5.

3.   See: **Sahih Al-Bukhari** (Bukhari's **Sahih**), English edition pub. in 9 vol. by Hilal Yayinlari, Ankara, Turkey, vol. 1, pp. v-vii; Rahman, **Islam**, p. 14.

4. On this period see: Ilse Lichtenstadter, **Introduction to Classical Arabic Literature,** N.Y.: Schacken Books, 1974, pp. 3-33; O'Leary DeLacy, **Arabia Before Muhammad,** London, Kegan Paul, 1927; Sabatino Moscotti, **Ancient Semetic Civilizations,** N.Y.: Capricorn Books, 1960, pp. 181-208; P. K. Hitti, **History of The Arabs,** N.Y.: St. Martin's Press, 1970, Ch. 1-7.

5. See Moscotti, **op. cit.,** p. 201 for more details.

6. Hitt, **Makers ...,** p. 9.

7. Hitti, **History...,** p. 114. For complete details of the trip see: **Sahih ...,** vol. v., pp. 142-148.

8. Hitti, **History...,** p. 118.

9. **Ibid.,** p. 123; R. A. Nicholson, **A Literary History of The Arabs,** Cambridge: The Univ. Press, 1969, p. 142; Rahman, **Islam,** pp. 30-33; Rahman, **Major Themes...,** pp. xi-xvi; **Sahih...,** vol. iv, p. 466, vol. vi, pp. 477-478.

10. Rahman, **Major Themes...,** pp. 1-16.

11. **Ibid.,** pp. 80-105.

12. On this see: Abdu L'Ahad Dawud, **Muhammad In The Bible,** Doha, Qatar, pp. 22-27, 51-59, 70-81, 88-92, 92-105, 139-140, 144-145, 147-151, 175, 189-191, 198-223, 236-238, 257-263; Jamal Badawi, **Muhammad in The Bible,** pub. by The Islamic Information Foundation, Halifax, Canada, n/d; Mohammad Chirri, **Inquiries About Islam,** Beirut, 1965, pp. 140-145.

13. Rahman, **Major Themes...,** pp. 121-131, 106-120; Sayyid Qubt, **The Religion of Islam (Hadha'd-din/This is The Faith),** Beirut, The Holy Quran Pub. House, 1980, pp. 30-31.

14. G. E. von Grunebaum, **Medieval Islam,** Chicago: Univ. of Chicago Press, pp. 108-141; Hammudah Abdalati, **Islam in Focus,** England: Derbyshire, 1978, pp. 29-30; Abdul A'la Maududi, **The Moral Foundations of The Islamic Movement,** Lahore: Islamic Pub. 1978, pp. 31, 40-45.

15. Summarized from Caesar Farah, **Islam**, N.Y.: Barron's Educational Series, 1970, pp. 112-113; Attar, **op. cit.**, pp. 97-109; Chiri, **op. cit.**, pp. 158-165.

16. See: Ignaz Goldziher, **Muslim Studies,** vol. 2, Gt. Britain: George Allen and Unwin, Ltd., 1971; Stanley Lane-Poole, **The Speeches and Table Talk of the Prophet Mohammad,** London: Macmillan and Co., 1882; Ahmad von Denffer, **Literature on The Hadith In European Languages, A Bibliography,** Gt. Britain: The Islamic Foundation, 1981.

17. On this see: Dwight D. Donaldson, **Studies in Muslim Ethics,** London: S.P.C.K., 1963.

18. **Sahih...,** vol. i, p. 29.

19. Abadalati, **op. cit.,** p. 37.

20. On Islamic slavery see: Bernard Lewis, **Race And Color in Islam,** N.Y.: Harper Torchbooks, 1971; Allen G. B. Fisher and Humphrey J. Fisher, **Slavery and Muslim Society in Africa,** N.Y.: Anchor Books, 1972.

CHAPTER FOUR

THE CALL

Approximately one hundred years after the death of the Prophet Muhammad, the Arab armies had expanded their power into the Byzantine possessions of the Near East and North Africa, had conquered the Persian Empire, and had brought their forces to the fringes of China and the vital limbs of Europe. For the Europeans, the Arab advance was observed as the last in a series of Caucasian tribal movements that destroyed the Roman Empire in order to inherit its former possessions. Seen from the Byzantine provinces, it was a liberation of sorts from the heavy taxes imposed by avaricious Byzantine officials and from the heavy-handed hold of a domineering clergy and church. Viewed from the throne of the Shah-en-Shah of Persia, it was violent conquest by rude, unlettered, barbarians whose only redeeming quality was their religion. From the seat of the Celestial Emperor of China, it was seen as a challenge for the domination of Western Asia. All this, and more, resulted from a call to the faithful of Islam to bring the world into submission.

Many reasons have been advanced to explain the amazing power and speed with which the Arabs carved out a vast empire, only second in size to the Roman Empire, and to explain its rapid collapse as well. It was, however, religion that acted as the cementing force that held that huge, highly sophisticated, empire together; and it was religion, again, that was responsible for its fragmentation and ultimate demise.

For as long as the Prophet Muhammad was alive, he was easily accessible to his people. He served them in many roles, as their prophet, as their head of state and, lastly, as God's (Allah's) legal representative on Earth. Shortly after Muhammad's triumphant entry into Mecca, he began the process of rejuvenating Arabian culture. All pagan practices were eliminated; the resulting culture became Islamic; and it was to become the "Classic ideal" for the future generations. A new state evolved.

At the head of the Islamic state is God and it is to Him that all allegiance and sovereignty is due. Next comes the Prophet Muhammad who received the Quran, the Sacred Scripture of Islam. The Quran is much more than a book of revelations; it is, and functions as, the fundamental and universal "constitution" of the Islamic World. It is theological in its Meccan chapters but administrative and legalistic in its Median chapters. Therefore, there is no separation of church and state in Islam; all warfare or conquest, whether offensive or defensive, is religious in tone, to "open" new nations to the call of the faith. War is either to protect or expand the borders of Islam. This objective is one of the major purposes of the Islamic state. The other major aim is to apply Islamic Law (the Shari'ah) to mankind. Islamic law is universal, for everyone, Moslem and non-Moslem alike, and it remains the primary source of legislation in Moslem states. It is believed that Islam came into being to replace all secular of non-Islamic nation-states, and to substitute them with Islamic administations and legal systems.

It should be obvious by now that secularism or secular institutions, as we understand them in the West, are viewed by Islam as meaningless concepts, at best, or as an enemy of God, at worst. Even an Islamic state cannot legislate "new" laws, for law is the domain of God, not man. Man can only apply or reinterpret laws by analogous means. Also, the concept of social sciences, subjected to experimentation and critical observation, is pointless folly for the Moslem, because all human activity - cultural, social, sexual, political, economic and even mental - must conform to Islamic principles, and be regulated under Islamic law, for the benefit of the human race. And, lastly, the concept of "humanism" or "universal human rights," as an aspect of the teachings of Christ, or as a secular quest, for human equality, are unacceptable to Islam. For the Moslem, a person's rights are those granted to him/her in the Quran, now and forever!

The law is the main instrument of the state. It insures that all who come under its sway live in accordance with God's will, subject to its rewards and punishments in this world and in the next. It sets the standard for the Moslem state by determining what is legal and acceptable and what is not. It is all consuming.

The origins of Islamic jurisprudence (**usul al-fiqh**) (1) are derived from the Quran, the customs/precedents (the Sunnah) of the prophet and his speech (the Hadith). In the course of conquest, new territories were taken and new problems emerged that needed legal solutions that the above sources of law could not resolve. New mechanisms were developed (2) to address that situation including a form of analytical reasoning (**qiyas**), personal judgment (**ra'y/ijtihad**), and a consensus of the community (**ijma**). Thus, the Islamic legal system came to fruition, but it was also criticized by some Islamic scholars who rejected some of the new innovations while others saw little that was new in Islamic law but, rather, they saw the system as a reflection of Arabian customs, minus the pagan malpractices (3). One of the two major problems in the administration of Islamic law is that it is extremely difficult to revise, because the law is neither historical or social in that it does not evolve from conditions that arise. It is prescriptive and, therefore, it leads the society into conformity. This feature produces tensions between divine revelation and human reasoning in the legal process (4), in interpretations of the Quran (5), and in the practical needs of the community. To characterize the Shari'ah as "God's Law" lends itself to another problem, that of human intervention in divine will, for unless God is the sole judge, prosecutor, defense attorney, and jury, in each and every case, it is extremely difficult to understand any legal decision as being God's, or even being based upon God's words, due to human intercession.

The importance of the foregoing discussion can be best seen in the rise of Islam and especially in the conversion of millions of people to the new faith. In time, Islamic law became the most potent force in the conversion of the non-Moslems living in Moslem states or under Islamic administrations. (The non-Moslems, protected at first by the early conquerors, were later stripped of most of their civil and legal rights.) In an Islamic state, the ideology of the state is Islam and, consequently, non-Moslems have no real place in the system, for they are outside the ideology of the state. At first, they were used by the conquerors but, later, they were seen as disloyal to the state and replaced by Moslem administrators. If one wishes to obtain any position of power, prestige, or to live in dignity, conversion to the true faith is necessary.

For Christians and Jews, there is a subordinate place in the Islamic state for them, as the dhimmis or Ahl al-Kitab (People of a Covenant or People of The Book). Their legal rights were modified, new churches could not be built nor old ones repaired, and they often faced severe problems, but, in general, they were tolerated.

The pagans were less fortunate. Seen as the "enemies of God," the pagans had the choice of conversion or extinction, but this was limited in some cases and impossible to achieve in others. Nevertheless, soon after the Moslem conquest, paganism vanished from its newly acquired territories. As the Islamic states solidified its structure, pagan temples were destroyed and pagan practices were declared illegal and terminated. The pagans were persecuted by the authorities, both overtly and covertly. Thus, Islamic law became the most potent weapon in the Moslem arsenal, for the faith.

Moslem women also faced some discrimination in legal matters (6), by western standards; their testimony was worth one-half of that of a man (7). Women were seen, and continue to be seen in some Moslem countries, as the possession of men, and a very well known hadith of the Prophet Muhammad states that even a lady's "milk beongs to the husband...(8)" Polygamy was limited to four wives, but concubinage continued. Since Islam forbids sexual relations outside of marriage or slavery, temporary marriages (**Mut'ah**) for the purposes of male sexual gratification were legalized, although the prophet opposed the practice considering it a form of prostitution. But, contrary to popular criticism and misunderstanding, Islam did grant women more rights than they had previously enjoyed in the days of paganism. The new religion protected women from infanticide, gave them rights of inheritance, allowed them to conduct business and to maintain their own wealth. However, the rights of women have not advanced much since then, under Islamic law, and the role of women, a measure of equality, has not changed much in many Moslem societies.

By the time the prophet had died, the Islamic state had been institutionalized. The question of succession to Muhammad's political role, however, remained open. Four parties put forth nominees for election as his successor (**Caliph/Khalif**), in his administrative and legal duties. The four groups represented the Meccans, the medinese Ansar (helpers), the Party of Ali

(Shi'a/Shi'ites), and a group favoring random selection from among all male believers. The Arabian Caliphate of the Rightly Guided (al-Rashidun) became the focus of political attention.

The first party succeeded with the election of Abu Bakr, the pious father-in-law of Muhammad, who was one of the earliest converts to Islam. His tenure in office (632-634 A.D.) (9) was largely occupied by the wars of apostasy (riddah), and the conflicts with false prophets such as Talhah, Musaylimah, and the prophetess, Sajah. Abu Bakr must be credited with ending all secession from Islam, by surrender or extinction. Thus, conversion from Islam is illegal and remains extremely dangerous.

Upon the death of Abu Bakr, Umar ibn al-Khattab was elected to the Caliphial post. His caliphate was primarily concerned with the Jews and Christians of Arabia. During the lifetime of the Prophet Muhammad, Jews and Christians remained in Arabia, although they were non-believers in Islam. (Had the prophet believed that the Christians worshiped or accepted more than one God in the Trinity, he could have easily destroyed them or evicted them from Arabia.) The Christians and Jews, however, were to pay a tax/fine (jizah) to the state and were seen as inferior to the Moslems. In return for the tax, they were protected.

When Umar went to collect the tax from the Jews, they refused to pay saying that they were Moslems in a sense, since they recognized one God and believed that Muhammad was a true prophet, but not for them. Thus, they did not reject Muhammad's prophethood, but only the validity of his mission for them. Umar, according to legend, became incensed, and ordered their expulsion from Arabia.

Upon going to the Christians to collect their taxes, Umar was confronted again by an attempt to end the taxation and to obtain equality for the Christian community with the Moslems. Apparently, the Prophet Muhammad was prepared to accept Christians who had acknowledged him as a prophet as Moslems who had "purified" their faith (10). But that was not good enough for Umar, for he wanted them to reject the divinity of Jesus and His crucifixion, and that, of course, the Christians would not do, becuse that is an inescapable conclusion of the Gospels. The Arabian Christians were willing to accept

61

Muhammad as a prophet, in the same sense they had accepted the Jewish prophets, but in no way would they compromise the divinity of Jesus or His death by crucifixion. (For them, Muhammad was simply one more prophet in the long line of Semetic Prophets. Obviously from this perspective, if Jewish prophets were to be honored by Christianity, then why not an Arabian one?

Umar could not tolerate the "arrogance" of the Christians and, apparently, he could not accept anyone, not even Jesus, being greater than Muhammad. His understanding of Islam must have precluded the divinity of Christ. Thus, the Caliph Umar reacted swiftly; the Christians were evicted from Arabia.

Of the most proud Christian tribes in the northern frontier, the Banu Taghlib continued to insist that to be a Christian one must have first been a Moslem, accepting God and His prophets, and then, in addition, His Son, Jesus. And, furthermore, they maintained their belief that Christianity was a complete and final revelation, separate from Islam and not subordinate to it. They saw nothing in Islam for a Christian, therefore, Umar took the sternest measures against them. The Banu Taghlib were forbidden to baptize their children, teach them Christian doctrines, and they were made to pay a double tax. some sources, however, indicate that the children of the Banu Taghlib were to be given the choice between Christianity and Islam when they grew older (11), but, eventually the tribe became completely Moslem since conversion from Islam is a capital offense.

Umar is credited with the total Islamification of Arabia, and later, his covenant was applied in the conquered territories. Succeeding Caliphates ended Umar's tolerant practices. The Christians of the Near and Middle East were taxed, the legal system did not favor them nor did it always accept their testimony, their properties could be confiscated as part of Dar al-Islam if they appeared disrespectful toward Islam or displayed Christian symbols in an unacceptable manner; new churches could not be built, and often, old ones could not be repaired. Christians in high places were eventually replaced by competent Moslems. (Only the mountains of Lebanon escaped the Islamic legal system, and therefore, Christianity flourished there and it generated a highly tolerant atmosphere, until recent events.)

Of the Jews in Medieval Islam, they fared much better than their co-religionists in Christiandom and, in many cases, better than the Christians under Islamic rule (12). The Jews, from a theological point of view at least, had fewer problems with their Moslem overlords, for both peoples had come to reject the divinity of Jesus and the Trinity. And, the Quran treats them negatively on only a selective basis.

The assassination of Umar by a Persian slave ended his caliphate in 644 A.D. He was succeeded by the worldly and sophisticated Uthman ibn Affan. During Uthman's reign (644-656 A.D.), he was accused of enjoying a life of luxury and of extreme nepotism. The opposition to his rule rallied around Ali who had been passed over three times for the Caliphate. Ali's supporters pressed his case implying that the prophet had indicated that Ali was to succeed him and, furthermore, that the prophet's family should be the only legitimate rulers of the Moslem World. Uthman's aids rejected the Shi'ite (Party of Ali) position believing that any Moslem could be the caliph. And, in fact, if Muhammad had chosen Ali to succeed him, then future generations might conclude that the Prophet Muhammad "used" religion to create a dynasty to rule over Arabia, thus the purity of his mission would be severely compromised.

When Uthman appointed a commission to revise the Quran, some of Ali's supporters accused the caliph of tampering with the text to enhance his authority (actually his family's position). Nothing Uthman could do or say could quiet the opposition; the political situation deteriorated and, finally, the rebels assassinated the caliph, in his home, while he was at prayer. His wife tried to shield him and lost two fingers to the assassins. The caliph's blood flowed over the holy Quran, soaking several pages.

Finally, Ali ascended to the caliphate (656-661 A.D.). Ali's involvement in the murder of Uthman may never be clearly ascertained. But, Uthman's nephew, Mu'awiyah, governer of Damascus, insisted upon punishing the assassins, and Ali could not or would not do so. The situation between the two men degenerated.

Ali faced opposition with Arabia as well; it was led by one of the prophet's wives, A'ishah, who had been slandered by

Ali in the past. With the aid of two companions of the prophet, Talhah and al-Zubayr, A'ishah led a revolt against Ali which, in the long run, failed. Encouraged by that success, Ali now became more adamant in his refusal to investigate the circumstances involved in the death of Uthman.

Mu'awiyah decided on more militant action which ultimately led to another civil war in Islam. The battle of Siffin (657 A.D.) ended the controversy. Ali led an Arabian and Iraqi force against Mu'awiyah's Syrian army. The inconclusive conflict convinced Ali to negotiate an end to the war and that, automatically, raised Mu'awiyah's position to that of a pretender to the caliphate. Some of Ali's forces, later to be known as the Kharijites, withdrew from the battlefield claiming that there should be nothing to negotiate. Thereafter, Ali had to make concessions; the fourth Caliph was assassinated by a member of the Kharijite group.

The death of Ali resulted in two great cataclysmic events. It shifted the political center of the caliphate to Syria and, later, to Iraq; and, it led to a major schism in Islam between the Sunnite Moslems and the Shi'ite Moslems (the supporters of Ali).

The heresiographical history of Islam can now be discussed against the preceding background. It can be classified into five basic categories; apocryphal Qurans, Sunnite and Shi'ite sects, false prophets, incarnationist sects and the Sufist (mystical) movement. All of these movements have a place in the evolution of Islam and all of them have influenced the present faith.

In perhaps the most potent form of religious, cultural and linguistic imperialism that can be recalled, the Arabians and Arabs conquered many peoples and assimilated a rich and vast intellectual heritage. They were also great scholars and innovators and, consequently, they contributed immensely to their subject peoples. Yet, they often faced revolts that were both political and religious in nature, for they used heavy-handed tactics in the quest to establish religious and cultural uniformity as well as political control. And, they treated the newly converted Moslems as clients (**mawali**), rather than equals.

The conquest of North Africa brought a large pagan group, the Berbers, under Arab rule. Although Caucasians like the Arabs, they were a distinct ethnic group with their own language and customs. They resented Arab domination, the attempt to impose Arabic in place of their language and, most of all, the attitude of the Moslem conquerors who viewed them as an inferior, "low," people.

Berber resentment broke out in the form of new prophets who received revealed Qurans in the Berber language (13). The Kharijite movement, now a sect, had taken root in North Africa (the Maghrab), and the Berghwata tribes had joined that schism about 744 A.D. The Berghwata chief Salih (al-Muminin), "the Upright and Faithful," was seen as, and proclaimed to be, a prophet by his people; he preached a revealed Berber Quran of some eighty chapters (suras). He must have proclaimed himself to be the expected Mahdi (14) - a messianic figure. Salih's grandson, Yunus continued the movement after his death. In the Rif region of Morocco, another man, Hamim, proclaimed another Berber Quran (15). This new prophet died in battle against the Umayyad forces of Spain in 927 A.D.

The Berber Qurans were an attempt to change the nature of Islam, not to do away with it or to start a new religion. To a considerable extent, they were modifications of the Arabian Quran but, perhaps, a bit more tolerate in spirit towards non-Moslems and non-Arabians. Not much more is known about them; they were, certainly, not unique but, at the same time, they may not have been forgeries either. As for Salah al-Mu'minin, apparently he was accepted by a large body of people as a prophet with a legitimate revelation; his followers maintained his movement well into the twelfth century; political conditions alone cannot account for his wide-based support. It is doubtful that he was a charlatan. The Berber Qurans, however, are considered apocryphal, that is unsubstantiated, by orthodox Islam; only fragments of them remain to this day.

We have already mentioned the Kharijites (16) in connection with their revolt against Ali. They were the first major religious-political movement in Islam, opposing the caliphate of Ali in favor of a more democratic process and a more puritanical regime. They maintained that belief in God and in Muhammad was not sufficient to enter paradise. Piety was the key; a Moslem who sinned was, in their eyes, equal to an infidel (non-believer). Kharijite doctrine has survived to this day in Oman, Tripolitania and Algeria. (They are known as the Ibadites in Oman.)

In response to the Kharijite creed which could excommunicate the sinful Moslem, the Murji'ites (irja/suspension) sect came into being. The Murhi'ites refused to declare sinning Moslems infidels, preferring to suspend judgment against them (17). This sect's hallmark was its tolerance of the individual and the political establishment, for only God has the right to judge Moslems, in their view.

To some extent, the Murji'ite doctrine was derived from another, older, philosophical school of thought known as the Qadarites. The Qadarites stressed the ability or determination of God in shaping things, but gave man human responsibility and free will. This movement did not develop into a formmal sect, but rather, it permeated many sects and orthodox Islam as well.

The most important following to develop among the Sunnite branch of Islam was the Mu'tazilah. The Mu'tazilite sect (18) began as a puritanical movement, supported the idea of free will, accepted rationalism along with revelation, favored separation of church and state to keep religion above the mundate politics of the day, rejected any understanding of the divine attributes of God (the 99 names of God taken from the Quran); and they took an in between position regarding the fate of sinners, neither supporting the Kharijites or the Murji'ites The greatest challenge they offered Islam was the rejection of the belief in the uncreatedness of the Quran. The Mu'tazilah maintained that if the Quran was co-eternal with God, that was enought to compromise His absolute unity (just as His having a Son could do). They supported the rational concept of the creation (khalq) of the Quran and their position won a wide base of support, until 848 A.D. when the caliph, al-Mutawakkil, refused to support them. Thereafter, orthodox Moslems would not longer be persecuted and, in fact, orthodoxy triumphed with the careers of Abu Hasan al-Ash'ari and Abu Hamid al-Ghazzali (19). Al'Ash'ari was the founder of scholastic theology (Kalam) in Islam, and al-Ghazzali proved to be Islam's greatest theologian.

While al-Ash'ari and al-Ghazzali were able to re-orient Sunnite Islam back to orthodoxy, the Shi'ite sects made an eternal rupture in the fabric of Islam.

The Shi'ite sect (20) began with the supporters of Ali for the caliphate. They maintained that only Ali and his descendants had the legitimate right to rule the Moslem community. All other caliphs were usurpers of the authority housed in the bloodline of the prophet, through Ali, his cousin and son-in-law. The Shi'ites accept the Quran, the speech of Muhammad, and the discourse and sermons of Ali, and the works of Ali's descendants as authoritative sources of the faith.

Although the Shi'ites did not succeed in establishing a state nor gaining control over the caliphate; they did, however, gain a wide following of malcontents, such as the mawali (clients) of the Arabs who were recent converts to Islam and, consequently, filled its lowest ranks. The movements expressed itself in religious terms, at all times.

The line of Ali descended through al-Husayn, to Ja'far al-Sadiq (d. 765 A.D.), then it split into two independent lines; one branch follows Ja'far's son Isma'il (d. 760 A.D.) and forms the Seveners or Isma'ili sects. The other branch proceeds to the twelfth descendant, Muhammad al-Muntazar (al-Mahdi/the Guide), who disappeared in a cave in 878 A.D., but who is expected to return to a victorious Shi'ite state. This group is known as the Twelvers or the followers of the hidden imam. All Shi'ite groups maintain the belief that in the absence of the rule of a descendant of the Prophet Muhammad, only the clergy should govern the Moslem World on his behalf. Thus, they reject the legitimacy of all rulers and political systems (with the exception of present day Iran).

The Twelvers (Ithna 'Ashariyah) became the main group of Shi'ite Islam and, although they swore allegiance to the caliphate of the Abbasids, they fared no better under its rule. They were distrusted because of their continued secret allegiance to the hidden imam (al-Muntazar) and their practice of hiding their true faith (**taqiyah**) while waiting for the return of the infallible Mahdi (also called al-Ismah) to come out of occultation (**ghaybah**) in the cave, in the future. The sect grew to power in Persia when Shah Isma'il of the Safawid dynasty declared Shi'ism the official religion of the state in 1502 A.D. The

Shi'ite clergy, however, did not accept the rule of the Shahs in place of their own and, therefore, they continued to plot against the state, achieving success in this century.

The only significant schism to emerge from this sect was the rise of Babism and Baha'ism which established the "Bab," Sayyid Ali Muhammad of Shiraz, as a prophet with a universalist creed. He and his followers were condemned by the Shi'ites and remain to this day a persecuted minority in Iran.

The Sevener sect (Sab'iyah) flourished in the Arab World in numerous denominations, known generally as the Isma'ilis. Due to space considerations in this study, we can only discuss a few representative movements but, nevertheless, these groups have greatly influenced Islamic thought to the present time.

The basic Isma'ili doctrine is based upon an inner (**batini**/hidden) or esoteric understanding of the Quran. The Isma'ilis were known as the Batinites by the "orthodox" Moslems, for the Isma'ilis claimed that only the allegorical interpretations (**ta'wil**) of the Quran were valid. The plain or literal meaning (**zahir**) was simplistic and insufficient at best to understand God's words. The students of this school of thought launched several movements against the establishment.

The first major threat to the Abbasid Caliphate of al-Mahdi was posed by a Persian, Hashim ibm Hakim, al-Muqannah known as the "veiled Prophet of Khurasan (21)." Al-Muqannah was a follower of Abu Muslim, a Khurasani, who played a major role in bringing the Abbasids to power. Ibn Hakim claimed to be a prophet and, later, to be divine. His disciples grew in numbers so that it took the caliph several years to defeat al-Muqannah's forces. The new prophet committed suicide, rather than surrender; but his followers became Batinites as he might have been; consequently, they supported several other movements against the state.

Hamdan Qarmat (22), originally an Iraqi, was converted to Batinite ideology and he began a campaign to convert people to his cause. He called for a form of equality under communal ownership which included wives and property, for the welfare of the group. He developed an allegorical text based upon the Quran, stressing tolerance and human equality, which included non-Moslems and pagans. His teachings reached the camp of the black slaves (the Zanj) of al-Basrah encouraging them to revolt under their leader, Sahib al-Zanj. The caliph responded to the Zanj revolution by ordering the extermination of the Zanjis. In the meantime, the Qarmatians founded their own state on the Persian Gulf and in 930 A.D., they seized the holy city of Mecca and stole the Black Stone from the Ka'bah. The stone was returned after the fall of the Qarmatian kingdom.

Although the caliphate succeeded in ending the Qarmatian movement, it met with a new danger from a poet and writer, Abu al-Taiyab, known to history as al-Mutanabi, the "self-made/self-styled prophet." Al-Mutanabi is best remembered for the excellence of his philosophically oriented poems. He died in 965 A.D., and his claim to prophethood was buried with him.

The Qarmatian crusade, however, did win many adherents, particularly in North Africa where an Isma'ili state was founded by the Fatimids. This sect takes its name from Fatimah, the daughter of the prophet and wife of Ali, thereby satisfying the bloodline requirement of the Shi'ites. Originally known as the Nizaris, this group flourished until the state was defeated by the forces of the renowned Saladin (Salah al-Din al-Ayyubi).

Military defeat did not end the movement; it survived and resurfaced in Syria in a new form as the Assassins of Alamut (23). The Assassins were led by the notorious Hasan ibn al-Sabbah (d. 1124 A.D.) who propagated his beliefs from his headquarters, the "eagle's nest," the famous fortress of Alamut. The sect's theological base was weak; it seems to have stressed self-interpretation of the Moslem Scripture, in batini form, with little regard for the role of the Prophet Muhammad. Sabbah's men ranged far and wide committing acts of terror and daring, derived from the use of hashish (narcotics). The movement was terminated by a succession of attacks by the Mongols and the Mamluk Sultan of Egypt, Baybars in 1272 A.D.) Today, the remnants of this sect are spread over Syria, Persia (Iran), India and Zanzibar and are sometimes known as the Khojas or Mawlas. They follow the present day leadership of the Agha Khan.

The Nusayris (Aliwites) of Syria are another important Isma'ili sect. They are named after their founder, Muhammad ibn

Nusayr, a ninth century scholar. This Shi'ite group believes in the incarnation of Ali - that is, that Ali, the cousin and son-in-law of Muhammad, possessed the Holy Spirit and, thus, he is divine. At present, they number about 300,000 in Syria (24), and they head the current government.

Another similar sect are the Druze of Lebanon, Syria and Israel. The Druze are an off-shoot of the Fatimid Caliphate of Egypt (25). When that caliphate ended, the followers of the Caliph al-Hakim, who believed in his deification, fled to Wadi al-Taym, in Lebanon, to escape persecution. They take their name from his missionary, a Persian, named al-Darazi. The Druze believe that al-Hakim is in a state of occultation, and that he will return someday.

In the Yamen, the Zaydi sect has survived as a moderate Shi'ite movement. Further to the East, the Shi'ite movement continues to grow. The Ahmadiya sect in India was established by Mirza Ahmad Qadiani (d. 1908 A.D.). This sect has spread into South East Asia and into parts of Africa. It rejects the Prophet Muhammad as the "Seal of the Prophets," claiming that the Quranic passage in question means that he is the "hallmark," of prophethood and not the last one; thus, they have maintained that Mirza Ghulan Ahmad is the awaited Mahdi, and a prophet for all Islam.

Other minor sects have emerged recently, some tied to Sunnite Islam and others to Shi'ism. In Nigeria, a new sect has proclaimed its leader, Mohammad Marwa, as the only true prophet of Islam. In the city of Kano, he worked miracles, he was shot at point-blank range by his enemies but the bullets passed through him without harming him, it is told. Marwa rejected the Arabian Prophet's mission trying to substitute his own version of it that would be black and African in nature. He was, eventually, killed; however, his disciples claimed that the world was not ready for him, so God took him back. He may, of course, return.

And lastly, the Black Moslem movement in the United States has drawn large numbers (26). They follow their prophet, Elijah Muhammad, and the sect has a decidely racial tone. Arab, Persian and Turkish Moslems have remained cool to their "revised" movement, saying that they are "fugitives from a reality in to a fantasy," assuming that Moslem slavery was somehow more benign than slavery under Christianity.

This brief exposition of the sectarian history of Islam shows the religion to be vibrant, flexible, versatile and innovative; it is anything but simplistic or monolithic. This study does not presume to debate all the complicated points of theology or philosophy behind the various sects or creeds. That has been done elsewhere for each group and, in fact, quite well. What has not been studied, however, is the religious rationale for the acceptance of those movements by a large number of adherents, and the inability of the "orthodox" leadership to purge them as heresies or an an aberation of Islam. In fact, most of the movements were terminated by military defeat, after the Moslem establishment proved to be ineffective in trying to thwart their polemics. (Orthodox Moslems have maintained, nevertheless, that God granted them victory over the heretics as proof of his favor, although the heresies still exist.

The only compromise orthodox Islam made with the non-conformists was the Sufi movement. Sufism (27), named after the wool garment worn by its adherents, was the only approved form of mysticism or Gnosticism acceptable to the Moslem establishment and, in some ways, it is clearly related to monasticism in Christianity. It did generate, however, a more militant form in North Africa such as the Almoravids (1056-1147 A.D.) and the Almohads (1130-1269 A.D.) (28). These puritanical movements grew and established cells throughout the World of Islam, under various names; but, nevertheless, they were controlled or regulated or directed by the orthodox Islamic establishment, in most cases.

The heretics of Islam justified their beliefs from the pages of the Quran itself, by their interpretations; thus, they appealed to the masses in terms they could easily understand. A look back at the earliest source of Islamic heresiographical writings, particularly al-Shahrastani's **Kitab al-Milal wa al-Nihal (The Book of Creeds and Sects)**, gives some convincing but not too detailed exposition of the rationale for the then existing heresies. The heretical movements seem to have several common denominators, taken from the Quran to justify "new" interpretations, new prophets, and the acceptance of the doctrine of incarnation. We may at least conclude for the present state of research, that in early Islam these concepts may not have been considered alien or forbidden to the faithful, nor strongly opposed by the establishment. Perhaps for this

71

reason, heresies still exist in Islam, despite the orthodox establishments utmost efforts to terminate all heresies, when they became mass movements.

Muhammad is clearly announced as the seal of the prophets in the Quran. His position remains, as always, unchallengeable but, apparently, some Moslems believed that being the seal of the prophets did not close the door of revelation within Islam. From that perspective, we can understand the rise of new prophets within the Islamic tradition, as men inspired by God to keep Islam on the proper path, after deviations occurred under the caliphates. None of the post-Muhammad prophets attacked Islam to form a new religion but, rather, they acted as modifiers of the faith, claiming authority given to them by God in the form of proper inspiration. They, in fact, acted as the lesser prophets of Judaism had done or, perhaps, as the Apostolic Fathers and prophets of the early Christian church. They were accepted because their revelations came in the mode or tradition of Islam and not contrary to it, often accompanied by a trance-like state. (From the establishment's point of view, the false prophets were all pretenders and any Qurans other than the Arabian one were fraudulent. This is a matter of dogma.)

The rationale for esoteric (Batinite) and allegorical (ta'wil) interpretations of Islam came from the Quran (Q 3:7) which admits its own ambiguity:

He it is Who sent down

To thee the Book:

In it are verses

Basic or fundamental

They are the foundation

Of the Book: others

Are Allegorical. But those

In whose hearts is perversity follow

72

The part thereof that is allegorical,

Seeking discord, and searching

For its hidden meanings,

But no one knowns

Its hidden meaning except God.

And those who are firmly grounded

In knowledge say: "We believe

In the Book; the whole of it

Is from our Lord": and none

Will grasp the Message

Except men of understanding.

No doubt, the "heretics" believed that they were "firmly grounded in knowledge" (of the Quran) and "men of understanding," consequently, they maintained the right to interpret the sacred text. And, nowhere in the Quran does it specifically state which phrases are basic (clear) and which have hidden meanings (allegorical/symbolic intents), or how many of them are subject to interpretations for a deeper meaning. The passage itself is extremely important for it gives the Quran a degree of flexibility for future occasions, although no-one, then or now, can claim to fully understand what the Quran says, for "no-one knows its hidden meaning except God." In reality, Moslems can never be absolutely sure of their beliefs but, also, this verse can act as the "elastic clause" of Islam, perhaps similar to the application of the "elastic clause" in the U.S. Constitution. Some more modern theologians of Islam have implied that the verse was intended to temper Moslem attitudes.

The problem of the "ambiguity," "unclear," "vague," "obscure," or "ill defined" characteristics of the Quran, was to be resolved through the process of exegesis (**tafsir**), orthodox commentary, on every page of the Holy Book, based upon the literal (**zahir'ite**) explanation of the text. The men who undertook this massive work, the mutafaserun, acted in response to ta'wil, and to give a uniform understanding of Islam to future generations. Their opinions are no stronger than those of their opponents, hence, heterodoxity remains in the Moslem World. In a way, the mutafaserun responded as the church councils had done in early Christianity - they established orthodox belief. Their right to interpret the literal text was exactly the same as the hererodox leadership, that is, based upon being "firmly grounded in knowledge."

The doctrine of the incarnation, meaning the possession by a human being of a divine essence or spirit, making a person divine, is contrary to Islamic belief. Muhammad made no claim to divinity; his humanity is very clear. He possessed his own spirit (ruh) like each and every one of us. A hint of incarnationist theology, however, exists in the Quran but only in reference to Jesus of Nazareth (Q 4:171):

> Christ Jesus the son of Mary
>
> Was
>
> An Apostle of God,
>
> And His Word,
>
> Which He bestowed on Mary,
>
> And a Spirit proceeding
>
> From Him: so believe...

The ambiguity of the passage revolves around Jesus being the Word of God, which only belongs to God and which places Him on the same level as the Quran itself and not Muhammad, and from "...a spirit proceeding from Him" which could be interpreted as "... a spirit of Him," because of the imprecision of the preposition, min (of/from), in Arabic. This controversy was decided when the commentators agreed to interpret the questionable phrase to mean that Jesus was a spirit proceeding from God, not God's spirit, coming into existence when God said the word "Be."

This explanation did not satisfy the dissidents of Islam in any way and, particularly, the Alawite theologians characterized it as nonsense, since it agrees with the obvious that we are all spirits from God. If not from God, they asked, then from whom? Apparently for the incarnationists in Islam, why should the Quran state something about Jesus that was already clearly accepted, understood, and obvious. The Quran upholds the holiness of Jesus, continually. Thus, they gave the passage a new and deeper meaning implying the possibility of an incarnation and the Alawites applied the theory to Ali, making him divine, possessing the spirit of God. The Druze applied incarnationist theology to several other prophets, as well. However, the Quran does not admit the possibility of incarnation to anyone except Jesus.

The success of the mutafaserun and of Islamic orthodoxy came to fruition in the eighth century when Abu Ja'far Muhammad ibn Jarir al-Tabari (838-923 A.D.) completed a monumental work explaining the Quran entitled, **Jami' al-Bayan fi Tafsir al-Quran.** His work became the trend-setter in Quranic exegesis, and it is still the basic work on the subject. With orthodoxy redeemed, the Islamic center of gravity reestablished, Islam was set for the future; and well set it was, for it became the world's second largest religion.

CHAPTER FOUR NOTES

1. See Majid Khadduri, **Islamic Jurisprudence, Shafi'is Risala,** Baltimore: The Johns Hopkins Press, 1961; Asaf A. Fyzee, **Outlines of Muhammadan Law,** Gt. Brit.: Oxford Univ. Press, 1955; Majid Khadduri and Herbert Liebesny, **Law in The Middle East,** Washington: The M.E. Instit., 1955.

2. On the origins of the additional sources of legislation see Joseph Schacht, **The Origins of Islamic Jurisprudence,** London: Oxford Univ. Press, 1959.

3. Mohammad Jamil Hanifi, **Islam and the Transformation of Culture,** N.Y.: Asia Publishing House, 1970, pp. 100-117.

4. Noel J. Coulson, **Conflicts and Tensions in Islamic Jurisprudence,** Chicago: Univ. of Chicago Press, 1969, pp. 3-7, 40-57, 58-76.

5. **Ibid.,** pp. 40-57.

6. A. J. Abraham, **Khoumani, Islamic Fundamentalists and the Contributions of Islamic Sciences to Modern Civilization,** IN.: Foundations Press of Notre Dame, 1983, pp. 12-13.

7. **Sahih Al-Bukhari,** vol. 3, p. 502.

8. **Ibid.,** vol. 7, p. 27.

9. Hitti, **History...,** pp. 140-142.

10. W. Montgomery Watt, **Islam And The Integration of Society,** Gt. Brit.: Northwestern Univ. press, 1961, pp. 260-261.

11. L. E. Brown, **The Elipse of Christianity in Asia,** N.Y.: Howard Fertig, 1967, pp. 30-35; Mahmoud M. Ayoub, **The Quran and its Interpreters,** Albany: St. Univ. of N.Y. Press, 1984, p. 166.

12. For more on Jewish-Arab relations see S. D. Goitein, **Jews and Arabs,** N.Y.: Schocken Books, 1970; Bernard Lewis, **The Jews of Islam,** N.J.: Princeton Univ. Press, 1984.

13. Charles-Andre Julien, **History of North Africa**, N.Y.: Praeger, 1970, p. 33; G.E. Von Grunebaum, **Classical Islam**, Chicago: Aldine Pub. Co., 1970, pp. 118-119.

14. Julien, **op. cit.**, p. 33.

15. Von Gruenbaum, **op. cit.**, p. 118.

16. Hitti, **History...**, pp. 246-247; Rahman, **Islam**, pp. 167-170; W. M. Watt, **Islamic Philosophy and Theology**, Edinburgh: The Univ. Press, 1962, pp. 10-19.

17. On the Murji'ites see Hitti, **History...**, p. 247; Rahman, **Islam**, p. 86; Watt, **Islamic Philosophy...** , pp. 27-35.

18. Hitti, **History...**, pp. 429-431; Rahman, **Islam** pp. 87-90; Watt, **Islamic Philosophy...**, pp. 58-71; DeLacy O'Leary, **Arabic Thought and Its Place in History**, London: Routledge and Kegan, 1958, pp. 123-134; A. S. Tritton, **Muslim Theology**, Gt. Brit.: Burleigh Press, 1947, pp. 79-106.

19. Hitti, **History...**, pp. 430-432; O'Leary, **Arabic Thought...**, pp. 208-225; On al-Ash'ari and al-Ghazali see W. Montgomery Watt, **The Faith and Practice of Al-Ghazali**, London: George Allen and Unwin Ltd., 1953; Duncan B. MacDonald, **Development of Muslim Theology, Jurisprudence, and Constitutional Theory**, N.Y.: Charles Scribner's Sons, 1903, pp. 188-192; A. S. Tritton, **Islam, Belief and Practice**, Gt. Brit.: Hutchinson House, 1951, pp. 103-108.

20. A. S. Muhammad H. Tabatabai, **Shi'ite Islam**, (Trans. by S. Husayn Nasr), TX.: ARM Press, 1979 is still the best introductory volume on the subject; Rahman, **Islam**, pp. 170-175; Watt, **Islamic Philosophy...**, pp. 72-105; Seyyed Hossein Nasr, **Ideals and Realities of Islam**, Boston: Becon Press, 1975, pp. 147-178.

21. Hitti, **History...**, p. 86; Tabatabai, **op. cit.**, p. 82.

22. On the Qarmations see Rahman, **Islam**, p. 176; Hitti, **History...**, pp. 444-446; Farah, **op. cit.**, p. 179.

23. On their colorful history see Bernard Lewis, **The Assassins**, N.Y.: Basic Books, 1968; Enno Franzius, **History of The Order of Assassins**, N.Y.: Funk and Wagnalls, 1969.

24. Farah, **op. cit.**, p. 183; Hitti, **History...**, pp. 448-449.

25. See P. K. Hitti, **Origins of The Druze People**, N.Y.: AMS Press, 1966.

26. Farah, **op. cit.**, pp. 274-279.

27. Still the best brief account of this movement is A. J. Arberry, **Sufism**, N.Y.: Harper Torchbooks, 1950; O'Leary, **Arabic Thought...**, pp. 181-207; Tritton, **op. cit.**, pp. 96-103; Hamilton A. R. Gibb, **Studies On the Civilization of Islam**, Boston: Beacon Press, 1962, pp. 208-218; Sir Thomas Arnold and Alfred Guillaume, **The Legacy of Islam**, Gt. Brit., Oxford Univ. Press, 1952, pp. 210-238.

28. See Roger Le Tourneau, **The Almohad Movement in North Africa in the Twelfth and Thirteenth Centuries**, N.J.: Princeton Univ. Press, 1969.

An Ecumenical Encounter

"Muhammad b. Ja'far b. al-Zubayr told me that when they" (a deputation of Christians of the Byzantine Rite) "came to Medina they came into the apostle's mosque as he prayed the afternoon prayer," (they were) "clad in Yamani garments, cloaks, and mantles with the elegance of men of B. al-Harith b. Ka'b. The prophet's companions who saw them that day said thay they never saw their like in any other deputation that came afterwards. The time of the prayers having come they stood and prayed in the apostle's mosque, and he" (Muhammad, the apostle) "said that they were to be left to do so. They prayed towards the east."

A. Guillaume
The Life of Muhammad
Ibn Hisham
Al-Sirat al-Nabawiyat

CHAPTER FIVE

CROSSROADS

The foregoing chapters have presented two "sister" religions of the Near East which have been, and continue to be, by their natures, dynamic, flexible, interpretative, able to accommodate varying national cultures, and lastly, meaningful for all times, places and conditions. The proliferation of sects and heresies that Christianity and Islam have spawned, at one time or another, attests to those factors and to their vitality. They represent crossroads in faith, converging and diverging in belief, yet always remaining within the monotheistic tradition of the Hebrew religion and the "heirs of Abraham." The points of convergence, to be sure, result from their common origin with the Semetic High God, and, certainly, not to eclectism; the points of departure result from the limitless intellects of their interpreters, and this, too, is more than just "playing with words." But, the words of scripture are the business of religion; and that is, to a great extent, all we have to rely upon.

For both Christianity and Islam, the image of God (Allah) in the world of man is similar, for it is the same diety; God the Father and Allah are understandably identical but the term Holy Spirit requires further elaboration. When Christians and Moslems speak of God, they reflect upon the same being, in most cases. He is a being, to be sure, not a virtual reflection of the mind or an imaginary entity. His characteristics are depicted in scripture and understood by Christians in terms of the "attributes" of God given by medieval scholars and, in Islam, by the ninety-nine "Names of God" associated with Him in the Quran. God is spiritual, as the Holy Spirit, while being anthropomorphic (1), possessing human physiology, seen most clearly by Christians in the Incarnation of Christ. (It is also interesting to note that only Jesus fulfills the ninety-nine names of God by word or deed/action.)

The Old Testament, the Gospels and the Quran reflect upon God's spiritual and physical natures; and of all His creations man is the closest reflection of Him, being composed of dust/clay for his/her baseness and a spirit for his/her loftiness and nobility, as depicted in the creation of Adam. Our concept of God is not only derived from Scripture, but it is shaped and defined, or perhaps, refined by the Scholastic Theology/Kalam of the Middle Ages. The methods of inquiry developed then put Christianity and Islam on the same path or line of thought, hence, it is not surprising that the image of God in both religions is quite similar.

The link between God and man is the prophet. From that perspective, it is clear that there have been major and minor prophets. We are concerned in this study with two major prophets, Jesus and Muhammad, because they passed through similar stages in life. Both Jesus' and Muhammad's lives hold blind spots that we know little about. Did Jesus live among the Essenes during the missing years of His life in the Gospel narratives; was Muhammad a Hanif and did he visit or live with them for some seventeen years that are absent from his biography. Perhaps so; it seems likely that a stage of earthly purification precedes prophethood and its mission.

Then, as prophets of the Semetic High God, they both faced a trial and temptation. Jesus was tempted by Satan while fasting (2) and Muhammad was seduced into speaking the Satanic verses of the Quran, during a false revelation, so as to see and praise the "daughters of Allah (3)."

Both Jesus and Muhammad ascended into heaven and they saw the fires of hell, as evidence for the existence and judgment of mankind, after bodily death. All that activity, and much more, was to confirm the rewards for those who possess a moral outlook on life, and to punish man for his/her ethical and moral malpractices while on Earth. The view of hell in the Christian and Moslem scriptures are similar - a flaming abyss; the picture of heaven differs to some extent. In Christianity, heaven is described in a spiritual sense, while in Islam, there is a more physical portrayal of paradise. In the Gospels, paradise consists of many rooms in God's mansion, but in Islam it is seen as consisting of seven layers or levels. The distinction between one room or level and the next is, perhaps, an indication or measure of faith, piety, and love of God and mankind. Thus, nearness to God is man's greatest achievement and it is inherited from actions in this world, as well as faith. It is also clear from the scriptures that the location of God's kingdom is outside of His creation, our galaxy or universe, since the Creator is outside of that which He created but, nevertheless, He may still intervene and interact directly within it, in order to alter His scientific laws of operation, to produce what we have called miracles.

Our knowledge of God and His kingdom are drawn from the sacred script of each religion. Here again, we see common problems and aspirations. The Gospels and the Quran are the fundamental texts for their followers and both are unique forms of literature for their time and place. In fact, they have no serious rivals today, although apocryphal "revelations" did appear, despite attempts at uniformity in both faiths. Historically, the scriptures of Christianity and Islam are valid for their followers today, as in the past. Attempts to debunk them have come to naught. Verification of scriptual events took place among the early apostles and companions of Jesus and Muhammad; today we accept those events based upon the faith, reputation and integrity of those individuals. Only the memory of the original transmitters of the Gospels and the Quran remain areas that cannot be fully verified. But, we know that those individuals made no claims or took no actions that could be construed as questionable or inconsistent with the basic dogmas of those faiths. Unfortuantely for us, neither Jesus nor Muhammad wrote down their own revelations, so we must rely upon the virtue of their disciples for the integrity of the holy texts. Jesus did pass on the guidance of the Holy Spirit to His apostles to inspire them in their work which became the biblical narratives (Luke 24: 44-53); and Islam relied upon the companions of the Prophet Muhammad in the composition of the Quran. And, lastly, it is possible that the "Q source" of the three Synoptic Gospels coincides with the "Book" that Jesus brought with Him that is mentioned in the Islamic Scripture.

The atmosphere and traditions into which the revelations appeared is yet another historical-theological factor that must be accounted for and understood. Revelation is a historical fact or phenomenon in that it took place in a specific time and place for both Christianity and Islam. It is not in the realm of "make believe," or "the once upon a time" of mythology.

The revelations of Christianity and Islam were witnessed to by numerous observers. But, also, they could not occur at just any time or anyplace.

Christianity came into a Jewish millieu, among montheistic believers who had become observers of the "laws of their God." Therefore, Christianity did not emphasize or deemphasize sacred law but, rather, it extended the law and altered the perception of the God-man relationship and human nature as well. It emphasized love, forgiveness, redemption and freedom from earthly punishment. It changed the sexual habits of mankind from lust to love; it made the naked human body a noble receptacle of the soul, no longer an object of guilt or shame. It fit perfectly into and elevated human nature as no other religion has done. But, most importantly, it gave mankind a fuller, more detailed, and clearer understanding of God in the Trinity.

Islam was revealed in a largely pagan atmosphere. The Christians, Jews, and Hanifi communities were not major forces in sixth century Arabian life. Therefore, like Judaism (4), Islam took a more legalistic tone, effecting punishments on Earth for "sinful" behavior, establishing legal codes of conduct ranging from acceptable behavior (ma'rufat) which is further divided into mandatory (wajib/fardh), recommended (matlub), and, finally permissible (mubah) to forbidden behavior (munkarat) which is sub-divided into hated acts (makruh) and totally forbidden actions (haram) (5). Islam maintains the possibility of the human body as a source of illicit sexual enticement and, in some sects, as an impurity for women, holding closer to ancient Jewish thought on the subject.

In general, however, it can be said that Christianity establishes a set of universal principles applicable to every dimension of life, while Islam is far more detailed on specific aspects, particularly since several revelations occurred to resolve a dilemma that the prophet faced, such as the number of witnesses required to recognize and try a case of adultery.

Furthermore, Christianity's world view differs from that of Islam's. Christianity made no distinction in attitude towards it followers and others, for all must be treated alike. There is one world and all people in it are a perfect reflection of the diety. Discrimination of any kind - religion, race, sex or slavery - is contrary to the teachings of Christ. We must all be able to play the same roles in life, as a measure of our human rights and total equality.

Islam's world view if more rigorously defined; a social structure exists based upon faith and sex. All Moslem men have equal rights on Earth but are actually spiritually identical in God's eyes, in heaven. They are followed by Moslem Women whose role differences establish their rights and performance capabilities. Christians and Jews follow in "nearness" or acceptabiity to Moslems, for they are to be, more or less, tolerated. Then come the enemies of God and the people outside the protection of Islam and, thereby, marked for conversion or extinction.

Islam divides the world into two great spheres, the Islamic nations where all citizens are subject to Islamic law and culture and the non-Moslem world upon which Islam has declared an eternal war. (To some extent, it is true that Islam makes war upon otherwise friendly nations and states that do not possess the true faith; and some Moslems living in non-Moslem states feel a degree of prejudice against them because they cannot live under Islamic law and impose it upon the non-believers.) Moslems, are at least in theory, if not in practice, the "keepers" or "caretakers" of "Allah's Commonwealth," and, as such, they have become the new "chosen people" of the Lord. From that perspective, this world belongs to its maker (Allah), and He has appointed and entrusted it to the Moslems to administer it for Him, under Islamic law. Therefore, there can never an an equivalence between Moslems and non-Moslems, for there is no equivalence between Islam and any other religion or ideology. Some devout Moslems believe that eventually Islam will replace all other ideologies and religions before the end of time.

Faith and state are irrevocably tied together forever in the role assumed by the Prophet Muhammad, and in the words of the Quran itself, if they have been properly interpreted. Nor should Moslems be loyal to secular states or ideologies (6), for secularism is irrelevant in Moslem eyes and, actually, hampers the spread of Islam.

And, lastly, it is clear that in the case of Christianity and Islam, the success of their respective faiths came with or

84

was associated with a triumph over a pagan city, for "God is Greater" (Allahu Akbar) than His oppressors. For Christianity, it was victory in Rome; for Islam it was the submission of Mecca. Furthermore, the conquest of Mecca established a model for the future of our world; purified Arabian culture became the culture of God and, consequently, Islam became God's plan for the future of mankind.

It is against this backdrop that we can discuss some of the more significant historical aspects of Christian-Moslem relations and, particularly, what came to be the accepted faiths of more than half of the population of this planet.

There are, at least, two lines of historical thought that must be investigated in the emerging relationship of Christianity to Islam. The first, which has been, perhaps, a bit exhausted by scholars, is the relationship that emerged when East and West met in conflict in the epic of the Crusades. That adventure served to heighten the already negative situation that had developed from the Arab conquest of Europe (7). By the time of the Crusades, the Moslem establishment had firmly rejected the divinity of Jesus, and the Crusaders, in a negative reaction or response, began to associate the Prophet Muhammad with the false prophets to come that are referred to in the Gospels. The Crusaders took a negative image of Muhammad back to Europe; it was embellished there (8), and maintained until this century. Unfortunately, contact with the West did not alter Islam's attitude or scholarship on the divine nature of Jesus. Thus, the two religions drew apart, until recent efforts at opening dialogue began in the last two decades.

Neither the Moslem nor Christian positions taken in the past were ever totally justifiable, even from their own scriptures, for those attitudes were derivative expressions taken from interpretations that were prejudiced by political conditions. (The nature of Jesus in Islam will be covered in greater detail in the next chapter.) The key issue at hand here is the parting of company between Islam and Christianity in the West. And, furthermore, the West remained cut off from Islam and the Eastern Christian Churches for many centuries. (After the Crusades, the West became embroiled in its own theological disputes in the ˋera of the Reformation, totally losing sight of Islam, altogether.)

In the Near East, new developments set the Islamic stage on a course of action which generated an Islamic view of Christianity. Firstly, the ambiguity of the Quran (9) required its interpretation in order to obtain uniform belief and, obviously, that process included all passages regarding the Christ and Christianity, although the final understanding of the Quran rests only with God as acknowledged by its interpreters. Secondly, the rise of allegorical (**ta'wil**) and hidden (**batinite**) interpretations challenged the orthodoxy's control over the Moslem people. Those unorthodox interpretations, some dating back to early Arabian Islam, were used at a later date to justify the rise of Islamic sects and, in some cases, indirectly involved Christianity. If seen from that perspective, they explain Islam's rejection of the Incarnation (**tajsim**), for all incarnationist movements in both Sunnite and Shi'ite Islam clearly justified their positions by citing interpretations, clear or allegorical, of verses in the Quran regarding the Holy Spirit and Jesus, and no one else (10). Thus, in order to reject the claims of the incarnationist sects in Islam, such as the Alawites, Druze, and others, it became imperative to reject the divinity of Jesus as well as the theology of Incarnation. This task fell to the interpreters of Islam, the mutafasirun (exegesists), but it should be stressed from the start that the opinions of those men were only one view that is purely human, without divine intervention or inspiration of any kind.

Also, and perhaps more importantly, there is no written evidence for the rejection of the divinity of Jesus in the Islamic tradition until some three hundred years after the completion of the Quran. The Prophet Muhammad, himself, lived among Christians in Arabia and, apparently, never accused them of polytheism, for if he had, they would have been eliminated, rather than protected.

The pre-mutafasirun interpreters included the Prophet Muhammad in his speech (Hadith), his cousin Ali (11), and the oral tradition of the prophet's cousin, Abd Allah ibn Abbas (d. 678 A.D.). Abd Allah is believed to be the originator of Quranic exegesis. (According to recent research, much of the material "related to his authority cannot be attributed to him.") As for Umar's view, relations and disagreements with the Christians of Arabia, nothing beyond the oral traditions discussed previously has surfaced.

The writings of the early commentators of Islam, if they existed, have perished. What we know of the opinions of Abd Allah and others is embodied in the work of Abu Ja'far Muhammad ibn Jarir al-Tabari whose encyclopedic compendium was completed in the tenth century, long after many Islamic heresies were hatched. It is impossible to ascertain if al-Tabari is reaching back to the past for justification or if he is simply rendering an oral tradition passed on to him or from exactly where al-Tabari has obtained his opinions. All subsequent interpretations of the Quran are based upon his work (12).

The Christian response to what became the orthodox Islamic belief about Christianity in the Arab World followed one of two paths. The lively debates that ensued between Christian and Moslem scholars during the Caliphate and afterwards were, for the most part, an apologistic polemic attempting to defend the Christian faith under intellectual attack (13). The Christians failed, in the long run, for their scripture, by that time, was considered to have been corrupted or interpreted falsely (**tahrif**), by either addition or omission; hence, their arguments proceeded from false assumptions, in Moslem eyes (14). There is, however, no evidence to support that accusation which arose to explain the apparent disagreements between the two religions. Similarly, Shi'ite scholars have charged tahrif against the Sunnite branch of the faith, indicating that the Quran has been literally alterned (15). The Sunnite defense has paralleled the Christian one, saying that the evidence is lacking.

In the Lebanon, however,the Maronite Partriarchate and their bishops took an altogether different approach to Islam which they saw as just another Christian heresy. They read the Quran with "Christian eyes" so as to interpret it in harmony with their own Christian beliefs. (The Maronite perspective enabled Christianity and Islam to flourish in amity until recently when outside interference upset the cordial atmosphere.)

The Maronites did not generate a formal school of thought or any literary tradition to support their views on Islam; in fact, most of their arguments were in the form of patriarchal encyclicals, or letters, to be read at Mass, by local priests, on topics of Christianity. (A few sermons still exist in the patriarchal library in Bekerki, Lebanon.) What the Maronite Church did that was original, however,was to build a systematic theology in defense of Christianity that was taken from old and new debates, in a rational manner, using the Quran itself as a source. Consequently, the Maronite Church lost few if any of its membership to Islam and, in fact, it won a few converts from Islam, including members of the prominent Shihabi family (who were related to the Prophet Muhammad's tribe.)

The Maronites maintained their religious integrity under a church policy of live and let live. They succeeded, to some extent, in reconciling the conflicting passages regarding the Christ in both Scriptures, seeing the differences as matters of interpretation rather than substance. What is known of their arguments and systematic analysis has been retained in the Maronite Church's oral traditions; they were passed on into Europe through contacts with the Vatican and the Maronite seminary in Rome. Some of their polemics were adopted by Christian writers in the West but it is extremely difficult to know which arguments were their own, which were taken from the Maronites, and which one's were borrowed by them from other eastern writers. Many of the Maronite polemics were adopted by the Dominican Order in Europe and faciitated the peaceful conversion of the Moslems of Spain annd Italy to the Christian faith, during the Middle Ages (16).

CHAPTER FIVE NOTES

1.   Q 5:64, 38:75, 39:67 refer to the Hands of God; 54:14 the Sight of God; 2:112, 6:52, 18:28 the Self and Face of God; 20:5 refers to His being seating upon a throne. Also see Sweetman, **op. cit.,** part I, vol. II, pp. 27-38.

2.   Luke 4:1-3.

3.   Q LIII:19-20. (The three pagan goddesses refered to were al-Lat, al-Uzza and Manet.

4.   See the interesting study by Abraham I. Katsh, **Judaism in Islam,** Block Pub. Co., 1954.

5.   For more on the legal and moral classifications see Abdul A'la Maududi, **Islamic Way of Life,** Stuttgart: Ernst Klett Printers, 1977, pp. 18-22.

6. On the rejection of secularism see Qubt, **op. cit.**, pp. 16-17.

7. Abraham, **op. cit.**, pp. 3-6.

8. Tor Andre, **op. cit.**, pp. 173-176.

9. Q 3:7; F. E. Peters, **Children of Abraham**, N.J.: Princeton Univ. Press, 1982, p. 111.

10. Q 4:171; They often concern the possession of the Holy Spirit by Jesus.

11. For this speeches, letters, sermons, and exhortations see the **Nahjul Balagha of Hazrat Ali**, pub. in Tehran, Iran, n/p. n/d.

12. For a representative list of both medieval and modern mutafasirun see Ayoub, **op. cit.**, pp. 3-7; 279-280. The list includes Tabari, Wahidi, Ibn Kathir, Qurtubi, Zamakhasari, Razi, Nisaburi, Ibn Arabi, Qummi, Tabarsi, Tabatabai, and Qubt. On the origin of tafsir see Peters, **Children...**, pp. 110-112.

13. Sweetman, **op. cit.**, part I, vol. I, pp. 66-68; 76-77. The major figure in defensive polemics and its major exponent was John of Damascus (d. 748 A.D.). His disciples continued his work and augmented it; they include Theodore Abu Qurra, Bishop of Harran (9th. cent.); Abd al-Masih ibn Ishaq al-Kindi; Yahya ibn Adi, the Jacobite (d. 974 A.D.); Hunayn ibn Ishaq, the Nestorian (d. 873 A.D.); Timothy the Nestorian Cathalicos (780-823 A.D.); Cyriacus, the Jacobite Patriarch of Antioch (793-817 A.D.); Abu Ali Isa ibn Ishaq ibn Zur'a, A Jacobite (d. 1007 A.D.); and Eliyya the Nestorian, Metropolitian of Nisibis (1008-1049 A.D.). There were others as well.

14. The chief advocate and exponent of this concept was the fundamentalist theologian Abd Allah al-Baydawi (d. 1388 A.D.) See Watt, **Islam and The Integration...**, p. 263; Geoffrey Parrinder, **Jesus in the Quran**, N.Y.: Oxford Univ. Press, 1977, p. 146. Parrinder's work is still the best single volume analysis of Christianity in Islam.

15. Ayoub, **op. cit.**, p. 36-37.

16. Abraham, **op. cit.**, p. 5.

CHAPTER SIX

IDEAS IN FAITH

This chapter is not intended to be a summary of Christian or Moslem polemics. It will, however, touch upon that subject only to ilustrate both Christian and Moslem interpretations of some Quranic verses. The intent here is to present both points of view regarding certain key issues as they are understood today; the objective is ecumenical (1), and to generate further study in that direction.

There is much in agreement between Islam and Christianity, nevertheless, the Quran presents only a brief view of Christ and, perhaps, an incomplete one at that (2). (The Quran's main thrust is directed against the enemies of God [the pagans] and not the Jews or Christians.) However, some Moslem scholars believe that the Quran is specific enough regarding Jesus for them to establish an image of Him that intersects but does not coincide with the Christian view. There is no doubt that in the Quran, Jesus appears as both a messianic and prophetic figure who proceeded Muhammad.

Of his birth, the Quran establishes without a doubt or question the Annunciation and conception of Jesus of Nazareth in a manner similar to Christianity; the virgin birth is reaffirmed; and the holiness of Mary is powerfully upheld (3). The unusual circumstances regarding the birth of Jesus, having no earthly father, is also established without doubt in the Quran but, in itself, it is insufficient to claim divinity for Jesus. Islam makes the case that Adam had neither a father or mother; Eve was created without a mother, and lastly, Jesus was created without a father (4). All this activity, it is said, is to demonstrate the ability and power of God in the creative act. The Quran views Jesus in the same light as Adam (5), as a pure creation from God, but not divine.

The Christians interpret these facts differently. Christianity agrees with Islam that God created Adam without the need

90

of parents, the most difficult creative act; thus creation with one parent is less difficult and, hence, it adds nothing to God's creative ability or power. Another explanation is, therefore, sought.

The Quran refers to Jesus as the Son of Mary, granting to Him no earthly father. This at least entitles Jesus to refer to God as His Father, in the absence of any other candidate; it establishes the technical competence for the use of the phrase, for Mary's chastity is absolutely upheld in both faiths. Furthermore, the relationship of Jesus to God (His Father) in the Gospels is amplified by God's own words calling Jesus His Son. God never refers to Adam nor anyone else in that precise way. We have no right to use that title for anyone else; we may all be the children of God, as a product of the human race, but sonship is a specific and not a general term, applied only to Jesus by God.

Also, St. Paul calls Jesus the "second Adam," in the sense that He was created by the breath of God as Adam was and not by normal biological generation (6). The Quranic phrase about Adam may also describe the soul-body relationship as a reflection of God - the unity of the base (body) with the noble (soul), in each of us. And, perhaps, of greater importance, the Quranic passage may elicit among Christians a response that the coming of Christ signifies a new beginning for the human race, in a spiritual sense, a second chance after original sin (a doctrine rejected by Islam), so that we can start over again in God's light, like a new Adam (after Baptism) - a sort of spiritual rebirth of mankind, according to St. Paul.

During the life of Jesus upon this Earth, the New Testament records that Jesus worked miracles. The Quran corroborates those miracles in numerous passages in "summary form" and as "signs," (aya) (7). These miracles include the healing of the blind, the sick, and the raising of the dead, as well as the fashioning of a bird out of clay and the breathing of life into it, (as God did to create Adam and an act that Adam was powerless to do). These are "Clear Signs" of God's grace. The Quran states that Jesus worked them as a sign from God in support of His mission, by God's "leave" or with God's "permission" (ithn) (8). In that case, God is the author and power behind the miracles of Jesus and, consequently, the miracles do not establish the divinity of Jesus or anyone else.

91

It is quite true that miracles do not establish the divinity of anyone. Miracles are recorded among Old Testament figures and the Islamic tradition offers miracles in support of Muhammad's prophethood. Some miracles have been attributed to the Apostles of Christ and to Christian saints, as well. Today, miraculous cures are still being recorded among Christian groups and communities, particularly at Fatima and at Lourdes. The real issue at hand here is whether or not Jesus invoked the miracles through His own power or whether He was only an instrument of God on Earth, and powerless to do them without God (The Father/Allah's) power.

The Gospels speak quite clearly about the miracles of the Christ. Christianity believes that Jesus worked His miracles in full agreement with God in heaven and, as an example of that, He spoke to God in prayer before raising Lazarus from three days of death. Hence, His works were always in agreement with the will or volition of God and that could be understood to mean that Jesus possessed the permission of God to do them. According to the Christian interpreters of the Quranic passages referred to, they saw them in agreement with the Gospel text that said of Jesus, "All authority has been given me in heaven and on the earth (9)." However, Christians also believe that the power to effect those miracles came from within Jesus, Himself, from His own spiritual force, identical to the Spirit of God residing within Him.

One may possess the permission of another to carry out a task, but lack the power to do it. Hence, permission and power are not identical or even equal. The actual power for all miracles resides with God alone. The Gospels clearly establish, however, that the power for the miracles of Jesus is contained in Him, quite unlike all other miracle workers, past or present, who believe that they have been the instruments of God on Earth. The distinction between the miraculous deeds of Jesus and all other faith healers is that the power for the works of Jesus came from the Spirit of Christ. The Gospel records that clearly and unequivocally. When a women seeking a cure for her illness was unable to attract the attention of Jesus, she touched His outer garment and "Jesus recognized in Himself that power had gone out of Him (10)," to effect the cure. His power, or better yet, the power of His spirit which Christians believe is divine (identical with the Spirit of God, The Father/Allah), manifested itself without anyone elses permission,

92

leave, intercession, or intervention in this world or from the next.

The greatest controversy to ensue between Moslems and Christians concerned the death and crucifixion of Jesus of Nazareth. Centuries after the Quran was completed, the Moslem commentators put forth a series of arguments denying the death of Jesus by crucifixion, based primarily upon their interpretation of chapter IV, verse 157 which reads, "...they slew him not nor crucified him, but it appeared so unto them." This passage became the dominant verse regarding the death (by crucifixion) of the Christ. Some Moslem scholars see that phrase as a rejection or "reinterpretation" of a historical fact or occurrence, and even as a negation of the divinity of Jesus, and the rejection of any "type of reincarnation," in the case of extreme Moslem sects. But, the early sources do not justify that perspective.

The first major attack upon the crucifixion of Christ came from the pan of al-Tabari (d. 923 A.D.) on the grounds of the nature of martyrdom as an "unfitting" and an "unnecessary," "blood sacrifice" for the "non-existing Original Sin" of Adam and Eve (11). The Quran and Islam, however, refer to both the death and resurrection of Jesus (12), and that should pose no problem for Moslem or Christian interpreters.

We have already indicated that Islam rejects the idea of an "Original Sin" inherited by mankind or derived from the disobedience of Adam and Eve. In the Moslem view, God forgave Adam for his sin, and thus, the innocent will not pay for the guilty. For mankind to inherit the transgressions of Adam and Eve would be unjust of God and contrary to His nature. Christian interpreters of the Quran agree that God forgave Adam for his sin but, also, insisted upon an act to balance the scales of justice befitting the insult to the dignity of God, resulting from Adam's disobedience; and, furthermore, a perfect sacrifice was due and it was executed by Jesus, on behalf of all mankind. For the Christian scholars, forgiveness was not enough, the insult or damage done to the dignity of God must be repaired or undone, by someone of the same magnitude as God. Man, with his imperfect nature at best, could not atone for the sin of Adam and Eve.

The nature of martyrdom is a far more complex issue in Christian-Moslem relations (13). The Christian view of martyrdom allows the individual to be overcome by his enemies so as to win a non-physical, spiritual, victory. Jesus fit precisely into that view, and He remains the Christian martyr ideal. The Moslem conception of martyrdom is more in touch with the physical reality of dying in the path of God **(fi sabil allah)**, so as to expand the physical realm of God on Earth **(Dar al-Islam)**, and to glorify the martyr **(al-shahid)** as a hero ideal. Clearly, Jesus did not fulfill that criteria and, hence, in the Moslem perception, His death by crucifixion would be understood as a humiliating end for the Messiah and a prophet of God. Nevertheless, by either criteria, Moslem or Christian, the death of Jesus should never be equated or associated with any pagan "blood sacrifice."

The possibility of both conditions of martyrdom being acceptable to God cannot be disregarded either. In the situation of Jesus, in Roman Palestine of the first century A.D., the expected Messiah could have been a martyr capable of fulfilling either criteria described above, from the Hebrew perspective. Jesus chose to be a spiritual Messiah and to be overcome by the reality of the moment for an even greater moral victory over sin and death. As the Messiah, He had to execute the plan of God and the prophecy of man, thus the road to the cross was preordained and necessary for the salvation of the human race. Not to die in the manner in which He did would have violated the Messianic prophecy as understood by His followers at that time, and to cast Jesus as an unsuccessful candidate for that role. The Quran, in referring to Jesus as the Messiah **(Masih)**, validates the conditions of Messiahship for Jesus, as indicated in the Old Testament and, consequently, may have established the conditions for His death on the cross. Had the Quran not used the word Masih to describe Jesus, then His death could have come by another means, although crucifixion, as an option, would still be a possibility among them.

The physical events regarding the betrayal of Jesus and His death on the cross are far more convoluted if studied from the Moslem perspective. Islam does not deny that a crucifixion did take place (14), at the appointed time and location. It raises the issue, however, that perhaps someone else, an Apostle, could have been crucified in the place of Jesus, in order to fit interpretations of verse 157 of chapter IV of the Quran (15). Since the literal reading of that passage establishes that Jesus appeared (**shubbiha lahu**) to be on the cross, or an appearance of Him was on the cross, several interesting hypotheses and candidates can be put forth for a "substitution theory." The Quran does not indicate that any substitution was ever made nor does it name any individual as a candidate; it only states that an appearance (paraphrased by Moslem scholars as a possible "look alike") of Him was seen on the cross.

The arrest and trial of Jesus poses no problem for either Christianity or Islam. Jesus was betrayed by one of His own Apostles, Judas; consequently, His identity at this point is crystal clear. After a brief trial, Jesus suffered the insults and physical violence from His torentors and, then, He was led along a path to His place of execution. It is during the trip to the cross that Moslem intellectuals propose a hypothetical scenario for the substitution theory. Accordingly, Moslems believe that God intervened "to rescue Jesus from his enemies" by raising Him to heaven for a period of "asylum (16)," prior to His return to Earth. So, who died on the cross?

Some Moslem scholars believe it was Judas, forced to pay for his sin against Jesus (17). Others say that Simon the Cyrene who had helped carry the cross was mistakenly crucified (18). Still others replace the Christ with Pilate (19). To a great extent, Islam cannot be held accountable for those inferences because many of them were of Christian design, and they had gained a degree of circulation in the **Heresies Answered** of Irenaeus. Most of those propositions were discredited long before the advent of Islam. Many educated Moslems no longer hold those views (20). In any case, a substitution theory would invoke incredible stupidity on the part of the Romans in order to lose sight of their prisoner on the way to the cross; and how could a person be so easily substituted for the bruised, battered and flagellated body of Christ without someone, anyone, noticing the difference. To explain away this obvious problem, Moslem psychologists and phychiatrists have, therefore, assumed that either mass "hysteria" (conversion disorder) blinded the Roman and others or a perceptual "hallucination" took place, by God's will. There is no basis for either assertion in the Quran or in anything the Prophet Muhammad ever said.

There are more plausible explanations, if the Quranic phrase in question is analyzed in a literal sense.

Docetic Christology, then prevalent in the Hellenic Near East (21), maintained that the Lord (Jesus) was man in appearance only, and that He only appeared to suffer and die on the cross. This philosphical school of thought was an attempt to disregard or downgrade the human nature of Christ in favor of His divine nature. The idea had gained some prominence among the Eastern Christian Churches. Perhaps the Quranic passage regarding the appearance of Jesus on the cross is a reference to Docetic Christology, rather than the "illusion" of a crucifixion. To some extent, Docetic Christology de-emphasized the physical nature of Jesus in that it asserts that He only appeared to be real, to suffer and to die. Although that doctrine was condemned by the church, it did not disappear quickly, but lingered on in the East, to explain the Resurrection and restoration of Jesus. From this perspective, chapter IV, verse 157, of the Quran does not deny the death of Jesus on the cross but, rather, it may be saying that His death was just temporary, not illusionary.

Moslem scholars raised another issue regarding QIV:157, specifically, who is the subject of the passage which reads, "They slew him not nor crucified him,...." Who does the "they" represent? There are three possibilities: the Christians, the Jews, or the Romans. The first possibility may be immediately discounted. The second group, the Jews, may be implicated by consent, but they did not carry out the execution. The Romans, on the other hand, fit the conditions of the sentence, and they, no doubt, believed that they had executed Jesus by crucifixion. Therefore, the passage does not deny the death of Jesus on the cross, but only that the Romans (who satisfied the conditions of the sentence, and thus may be its subject) believed that they had killed Jesus. His Resurrection proved them wrong.

Western scholars have maintained that the subject of the sentence was the Jews and the passage only denies that the Jews killed or crucified Jesus, which is also true (22). The Christian Chruch often considered the Jews guilty for the death of Jesus and, in the Middle Ages, labeled them the "Christ Killers." Perhaps the Quran is anticipating those charges and is meant to remove the blame and guilt form them, as Jesus, Himself, had done.

That Jesus did die on the cross is obvious. Crucifixion, the physical process in and of itself, may not be the most efficient method of execution. And, furthermore, some Islamic scholars point out that it may take "days for a person to die on the cross." This is remotely possible, even it if is not probably, and, therefore, true. Even before Islam, however, some Jewish scholars had argued that Jesus could have been drugged (Mark 15:23) and, later, revived by His associates.

According to the Gospel accounts, Jesus did die on the cross. Death came from asphixeation, the lungs filling with liquid from one's inability to breath while hanging from the crossbar. As a test of that agonizing, and deliberately inefficient method of execution, the Gospels record that a Roman soldier, in order to ascertain that death had transpired, plunged his spear into the side of the Messiah, the Roman test to puncture the lungs and draw out the liquid. The body of Jesus was then placed in a sealed cave, and it was guarded by the Romans to prevent its theft.

When Christ first appeared to His followers after His earthly demise, He was not immediately recognized by them. He had passed through a stage of tranformation from death to life. He was seen in the process of refusion, body and soul. The physical Christ was indeed different, the bruised body and scourged flesh was fully healed. In that moment, when the divine spirit of Jesus picked up His human body, cold with death for three days, He rose to heaven and, then, returned to our world whole. This event is one of the greatest teachings of Jesus. In heaven we will know one another as on Earth, but without the physical deformities that effected us here. Illness, suffering, retardation, and deformity have no place with Christ in His Father's kingdom. The consequences of crucifixion left no mark on Him, other than those He chose to keep, after the Resurrection.

There were, however, several marks left on the body of Christ, for a positive, unmistakable, identification. The nail marks in His wrists which had held Him fast to the cross were still there, as were the nail marks on His feet. And, more importantly, the stab would in His side, left there by the soldier's lance, was clearly evident. Even a doubter like Thomas could no longer doubt the physical Resurrection of his Lord and Master.

But, could an identical twin brother of Jesus have been substituted for Jesus, ask some doubters. Perhaps, but there is no evidence for that assumption. How could an identical twin brother exist and be kept secret for some 33 years in a small community, anticipating the crucifixion of Jesus, without anyone knowing about it. And, how could that person fool the Apostles and others who knew Christ so very well, had intimate knowledge of Him, and could have quite easily unmasked a charlatan, with or without self-inflicted, masochistic, holes in his body.

It is true that Jesus often referred to His cousin James as His brother, but He did so as a common term of endearment used among the Semetic peoples of the Near East. And, both Jesus and James were there at the same time; and, James remained in the area after the Ascension. They could not have been confused as one person playing two roles or two persons playing one role, or anything else. The Apostles of Christ were no fools; they fully understood what was happening, so let us not make doe-eyed emotionally disturbed imbeciles out of them.

Obviously, two major points of disagreement between Christianity and Islam revolve around the divinity of Jesus and the doctrine of the Trinity. Islam vividly presents two powerful and insightful categories of polemics against the divinity of Christ. The first line of thought rejects the Incarnation (**tajsim**) of Jesus for that was seen as "bringing God down to the level of man (23)," something that is not really meant or intended by Christianity. In Islam, it is believed that God and man are absolutely dissimilar, they cannot mix or one would be confused with the other. This early Moslem argument merits greater understanding. The Jewish view is also similar, and makes a very strong case for the same point. In this respect, both Judaism and Islam share common ground and are in agreement.

For Christianity, the distinction indicated above is not as clear or as simple. In Judaism, God is seen as possessing a throne, a court, and He even prays to Himself so that His mercy prevails. He created man in His image which is both spiritual and physical. The Quran, also, attests to God being seated on His throne, having eyes, hands, and a face. The implication is clearly more than just a spiritual essence and nature, for it implies a physical one as well. The ultimate projection of the corporal reality of God is in the Incarnation of Christ. God is a real, living, person who is eternal. He is incarnate, already, even before the birth of Jesus.

Some Moslem scholars have elaborated further, however, by accepting the physical reality of God, while rejecting the divinity of Jesus, or any other earthly person. They base the polemic squarely upon a Quaranic passage implying that it is below the dignity or majesty of God to take to Himself a son (24), for God has no need of any other person, place or thing.

From the Christian perspective, the above passage reflects an "adoptionist" theology which they, themselves, had rejected. That is why Christianity uses the term "begotten, not made, one in being with The Father..." to show continuity in the relationship between God and Jesus. The biological Christ was a unique creation of God. The Quran refers to Jesus as being "supported" by the "Holy Spirit," and that God cast "His Word" upon Mary and gave her a "Spirit from Him." Moslems interpret the Holy Spirit in this passage to be Gabriel; the Quran does not say that. Where ever Gabriel appears in the Quranic text, he is clearly mentioned by name. (In an early Persion commentary (Sharh) on the Quran, the Tafsir-i-Husaini, the Holy Spirit is associated with the Holy soul of Jesus, the Gospels, the name used by Jesus to raise the dead, and the angel Gabriel.)

In the Christian view, there is no theological justification to confuse Gabriel with the term for the Holy Spirit in the Quran. But, even if this substitution for the third person of the Trinity were acceptable, Jesus is still depicted in divine terms in the Quran, as the "Word of God," which belongs only to God, and as a "Spirit from/of Him," which also belongs to God. There is no reason to assume that Jesus was an evil spirit and, therefore, not from God; and, also, no justification to state the obvious, that He was, unless it establishes for Him and Him alone a special, significant, spiritual relationship to God, His Father. In this case, the controversy revolves around the meaning of the words "Holy Spirit," and the uniqueness of that spirit, as manifested within the body of Christ.

And lastly in this regard, there is a verse in the Quran (Q 5:17) that reads, "they have disbelieved who say that God is the Messiah, son of Mary." Many Moslems understand this phrase to imply a direct denial of the divinity of Jesus. But, a Christian would read it as an affirmation of the Father-Son reality between God and Jesus, in order not to confuse the two beings as one. The Messiah is the Son of God, by God's own command, - "This is my beloved Son" - but, God The Father is not the Messiah. This is a technical correction aimed at the Christian heretics of the period, not a denial of the divine nature of Christ. Jesus is the Messiah, the Son of God, by Mary. He is divine, therefore, also God, but not God the Father, thus they are two separate persons. God, in the passage cited, refers to Allah, or in Christian terms, God the Father. To say that God is the Messiah is confusing, creating one person for what is intended in the Trinity.

In addition to the foregoing discussion on the divinity of Jesus, there are several supplementary arguments of recent scholarship that bear comment, due to their insightful nature. They, in general, rely upon Matthew's text in the Gospel and not upon any Quranic inferences. They are, then, of course, of a different nature than the preceding thought and presume to show that the Gospels deny the divinity of Jesus. These arguments propose to show more recent commentary on the Gospels by modern Moslem scholars.

The temptation of Jesus (Mt. 4:1-11) is interpreted as an indication of the humanity of Jesus, for how could the evil force challenge God who is far superior to it. The Christians interpret the event as a temptation of only the biological, human, nature of Christ, to show His full humanity; but the rejection of the act of temptation is by His divine nature, for He says "You must not put Jehovah your God to the test," thus identifying Jesus with Jehovah by whom the test (temptation) was rejected.

In Matthew 15: 21-28, a passage describing a Phoenician woman's request for aid from Jesus, Moslem scholars see His response as indicative of "ungodly" behavior (lacking in mercy, discrimminating against her and, finally being won over by a polytheist). Christian interpreters see in this verse a lesson to be learned against the prejudice of the times by the "closed" Jewish community toward the pagans. Faith in God can save a pagan, even if they were not members of the Jewish community. Anyone may be saved if they accept God, even those as "low as dogs." Even though the mission of Jesus began in the Jewish nation, this passage illustrates that it was for all mankind, from the very beginning.

In regard to the will, volition, of Jesus and God, Matthew 7:21 is cited by Moslem scholars to establish the subservience of Jesus to God; and Matthew 14:23 indicates that Jesus prayed to God in supplication. However, the first citation indicates that belief in Jesus as the Lord is not sufficient to enter paradise, unless one does the will of His Father as well. The passage establishes Jesus as Lord but, also, as One who requires the commands of His Father to be upheld and obeyed. There is unity in volition within the persons of the Trinity. As far as prayer is concerned, the Old Testament tradition believes that God prays to Himself and He even studies the Torah and Mishna (25). In the Christian faith, Jesus prays publically in order to instruct others in what to say and privately as speech to His Father, as any good son would do. Prayer is not resticted to "submission" or "supplication" in Christianity, but, rather, it is man's right to address His God, directly.

From Matthew 27:7-8 and 27:46, Moslems make the case for restricting the role of Jesus to that of a prophet, subservient to God's will. From the Christian perspective, the Gospels establish the predestiny of Christ as a separate person within the Trinity. Jesus, Himself, indicates that He was born for a special purpose of God.

The "last hour" that Jesus spoke of also raises an important issue in theology (Mt. 24:36). Why does God, the Father, not wish to reveal the last hour of the end of time, to Jesus? Jesus chooses not to question or reveal that time to His disciples so as to exercise the power of faith over human behavior. It is God, the Father's prerogative not to reveal that hour to Jesus, for if He had then the life and mission of Jesus could become null and void, for a special few could falsely prepare themselves for the end, knowing precisely when it would come. Thus, we must always be prepared to meet our individual end-time, never knowing when it will occur. It would also be contrary for Jesus not to reveal it, if He indeed knew it, for that would then lead to a divine deception. Hence, Jesus rejects that knowledge, as part of His humanity, keeping it within the realm of His Father's intellect by choice, a choice which is clearly His.

101

Other scholars ask why was Jesus forsaken on the cross? Was that necessary and would God really forsake those (the prophets) He loved? The crucifixion scenario involved those aspects as well as others, in order to maintain that Jesus died a lonely human death of His own free will, not participating in a fradulent or illusionary act of mortality. It was important because He forgave His tormentors from that forsaken position as an act of man, done by One who was divine and could have stepped down from the cross to destroy His enemies.

And, along this line of questioning, one last, but extremely insightful, point has been made by Moslem scholars. In John 20: 16-17, Jesus establishes that He must ascend to heaven, to His God. This passage, according to Moslem thinkers, clearly shows that Jesus referred to God in heaven as His God, maintaining the unity of that person. Thus, Jesus has a God and, consequently, cannot be God. Christian scholars interpret that passage differently. In it, Jesus acknowledges His Father in heaven to whom He must ascend and that verse, therefore, gives a clearer, more in-depth, and precise view of the nature of God, as part of the Trinity. It does not negate the divinity of Christ, but acknowledges His reunification with His Father in heaven.

The Trinity now becomes the key to understanding the full nature and essence of God. It is purely a Christian concept or, perhaps "misconception," or has it always been evident in God's revelation to mankind? And, what does it mean?

We have already referred to the term Trinity in this chapter without the benefit of further elaboration. The term itself does not appear in either the Gospels or in the Quran. It was developed to describe the essence and nature of the Semetic High God of Judaism, Christianity, and Islam in the most exacting, in-depth, and clearest way possible, without associating Christianity with any other polythestic belief, of any number. We have stated in clear precise terms that Christianity was uncompromising nonotheistic, as are Judaism and Islam. But, stating the obvious did not automatically rule out the possibility of confusion in the human mind. Thus, to avoid any possible misconception regarding what Christians should believe, a short-hand term, the Trinity, came into existence to give the most vivid, most accurate view of God, for all mankind. In this perspective, it stands for the three manifestations (**muzaharat**) of God maintaining a "composite" unity (**tawhid**) of the Father, Son and Holy Spirit of one essence and nature (26).

The Quran, as previously indicated, rejects polytheism and pantheism. It clearly states:

Assuredly they have disbelieved

who say: "God is one of three."

(or a third of three) Q 5: 72-77.

And:

O people of the Book! Do not

exaggerate in your religion nor

utter anything concerning Allah

except the Truth...So believe in

Allah and his messengers, and do

not say three - Stop (it is) better

for you! Allah is only one. Q 4: 171.

Obviously, there is a condemnation of polytheism in the form of tri-theism in those verses. But, why and how did they become associated with the Trinity of Christianity is extremely questionable, for there are more plausible explanations for the verses quoted.

Moslem scholars included Christianity in the proscription implied in the foregoing passage, but they also raised questions anew. Who does the "they" represent? There are several possibilities. The pagan Arabian religion included the belief in astrial triads, and those people could have been the subject of the passage. Also, Hindu tri-theism had manifested itself in the Arabian peninsula resulting from the Indian Ocean trade complex.

The second passage is, however, addressed to Christians, but not necessarily against Christian beliefs. In that verse there are two historical perspectives that must be addressed. The first involves the Satanic passage (Q 53: 18-20) in which Satan put into the prophet's mind a few words of praise for the three Arabian goddesses (al-Lat, al-Uzza an Manat), according to the historian and Quranic commentator al-Tabari (27). The pagans present understood the phrase to be a reconciliation attempt between themselves and the Moslems. News of that arrangement soon reached Aybssinia, and the proposed reconciliation between the Qurayshi pagans and Muhammad sent the Moslem immigrants there back home, according to Ibn Ishaq. It is highly possible that the warning quoted above was addressed to the Christians of Arabia to reject an Islamic "trinity" composed of the three "sisters" of Allah.

Another possibility also exists. According to the prophet's biographer (28), Ibn Ishaq, Muhammad warned the Christians regarding a trinity composed of God, Jesus and Mary (29). This heresy, apparently, originated with the Borborians of Armenia and/or with the Collyridians of Arabia. Obviously, Muhammad could have easily come into contact with those ideas and, consequently, the trinity Muhammad and the Quran condemn is certainly not the Trinity of Christianity.

Christianity maintains that the concept of the Trinity, explicitly stated in the Gospels as Father, Son and Holy Spirit, is implicitly stated in the Old Testament and in the Quran, for the Trinity is eternal. It is not meant to be solely a Christian concept.

In the Old Testament, in Genesis, there is an impliction of plurality in reference to God. The Hebrew word for God, Elohim, is interpreted as the plural form of Eloah. And, the oneness of God, the word for His unity, echad, has been used in the plural, according to some scholars. Also, God said, "Let us make man in our likeness (image)" as translated from Gen. 1:26. Thus, God speaks of Himself in the plural. The diversity within the unity of God is not clearly indicated as a Trinity here, but, obviously, the passage pre-dates the coming of Christ.

In Christianity, the Gospels clearly expand and state the Trinitarian formula, thereby limiting the plurality concept within monotheism to exactly the three persons of the Trinity.

Christians would probably say that their faith in the Trinity is not a break with Judaism or Hebraic monotheism but, rather, an expanded, more complete and more accurate, or more detailed understanding of the Semetic High God.

In Islam, the absolute unity of god is potently upheld, as in Judaism, but the Quran, like the Torah, implies a plurality in reference to Allah:

"We will make him a sign to men..."

God says: "We have done, We have

commanded, We have created an We

have decreed, "and they say, If He

were one he would have said I have

done, I have created, and so on...(30)"

The above question was posed to the Prophet Muhammad by a Christian delegation.

The Prophet's response was a clear and concise reply emphasizing the unity of God. He did not, however, criticize the Christian Trinity. It is obvious that God spoke in the third person plural, in keeping with Christian dogma. But, he reaffirms His unity (**tawhid**) for God (Allah/the Father) speaks for all three persons of the Trinity in the Quran, perhaps in complete unity with one another depicting one will and one voice, now reunited in heaven. That in no way denies the three persons of the Christian Trinity.

At a later date, some Moslem scholars tried to explain away the obvious literal "We," in order to eliminate any hint of a Trinity in Islam. Al-Tabari, in his authoratative exegesis of the Quran, suggests that perhaps the "We" should be understood as a singular, as in the case of a "majestic we." When a king or president speaks for a nation, for example, he may speak as an individual but use the plural form we.

The "majestic we," however, created a further problem for future scholars. A king or president using the plural form of address is contingent or dependent upon those for whom he is speaking and, thus, a dependency problem exists. God is not dependent on anyone or anything. He is the eternal "I." The majestic "We" in this case clarifies nothing; it simply restate the composite unity of God.

Subsequent Moslem scholars have abandoned Tabari's position as "undefendable" but argue, in its place, that the "We" used by God in the Quran is not intended to be a personal pronoun. In that case, it represents an authentic Moslem formula for a trinity indicated in the Holy Book of Islam, in the opening sentence of each chapter, with the exception of one (31). This Islamic trinitarian formula reads, "In the name of God (Allah), the Merciful (al-Rahman), the Compassionate (al-Rahim)." Apparently, the phrase is meant to reflect the Christian profession of faith that preceeds or is part of each prayer that reads, "In the name of the Father, the Son, and the Holy Spirit." Thus, they may both represent manifestations of the same, eternal, Semetic High God.

Furthermore, the first part of both formulas presents no problem, Allah and God the Father are understandably one and the same person. The equivalence of "Son" with "the Merciful" and "Holy Spirit" with "the Compassionate" represent a unique problem, and an ingenious one, in Islamic analytical reasoning. "God's mercy as Rahman encompasses the entire creation, whereas His compassion as Rahim is limited to His faithful servants." Therefore, one could also say that Rahman is in both this world and in the world to come or He who causes existence (as the Father caused the Son), and Rahim with regard to only this world or the ideal perfection of the human specie (as were Jesus and Muhammad, His faithful servants) (32). If this were the case, then, perhaps, the Christian Trinity should read, In the name of the Father , the Holy Spirit, and the Son.

However, Christian and Moslem scholars could reverse the above analogy to conform with the original Christian trinitarian formula. (This is not as difficult a change as it may seem because the tri-literal root of both Rahman and Rahim (r, h, m) are the same.) In that case, "He is Rahman (merciful) of this world and Rahim (compassionate) of the next, because His mercy in this world included the rejectors of faith as well as the faithful and reprobates, as well as the righteous, while

106

in the next it is limited to the faithful (33)" (who are in heaven). Consequently, Rahman (in this world and in the next) would represnt Jesus (who lived in both), while Rahim (in the next, heaven) is limited to the Holy Spirit. If this analogy holds, then as a reunited Trinity in heaven, al-Rahman holds the "unity of attributes" and al-Rahim holds the "unity of action" as manifested in both Christianity and Islam. An interesting analogy!

The foregoing discussion is intended to be an introduction to the fascinating and highly complex study of Christianity and Islam. It is not an in-depth review of polemics but, rather, the study is designed to show differences of interpretation an understanding. Understanding is the key, the goal, to help foster the spirit of toleration and love between Christians and Moslems. The perspective of this study is ecumenical and to generate further research and writing in the fascinating field of comparative religion and in Islamics.

There are many, however, who may radically disagree with the findings of this study, perhaps, heartily so, but I assure the readers that this academic exercise holds no subterfuge to fear, for it takes no side. Those who honestly disagree are always welcome to respond to any issue I have raised in their own works. "For God knows best."

CHAPTER SIX NOTES

1.   For recent dialogue in this direction see **Jewish, Christian, Muslim Dialogue**, ed. by Leonard Swindler (**Journal of Ecumenical Studies**), vol. xiv, no. 3, Summer, 1977; **Islamic Christian Dialogue**, Libya, Tripoli, 1976.

2.   Muhammad Ata ur-Rahim, **Jesus, A Prophet of Islam**, London: MWH Pub., 1979, p. 206. This book contains an excellent summary of the passages in the Quran that refer to Jesus (pp. 207-220), and Jesus as seen in the Hadith (and Sunnah) of Islam (pp. 221-229).

3.   Q 3: 42-53; 19: 16-36; Parriner, **op. cit.**, pp. 67-74.

4.   Abdalati, **op. cit.**, pp. 171-172; Parrinder, **op. cit.**, pp. 69-70.

5. Q 3: 52-59.

6. Alfred Guillaume, **Islam**, Baltimore: Penguin Books, 1964, p. 196.

7. Q 5: 109-117; 3: 43-51; Abdalati, **op. cit.**, pp. 176-177.

8. Abdalati, **op. cit.**, pp. 176-177; Parrinder, **op. cit.**, pp. 83-91.

9. Matthew 28:18. Authority here may be understood as a rough equivalent of the Arabic word for permission used in the Quran.

10. Mark 30:21-43, (specifically versis 30-34).

11. Abdalati, **op. cit.**, pp. 179, 183.

12. **Ibid.**, p. 182. According to Abdalati and others, Jesus reappeared after a period of "asylum." On the death of Jesus see Q 19: 33,34; 3: 48, 55; 5: 75, 79.

13. Wilfred C. Smith, **Islam in Modern History**, N.Y.: The New American Library, 1957, p. 37 (f.n. 27) touches upon this extremely important issue.

14. Abdalati, **op. cit.**, p. 178.

15. **Ibid.**

16. **Ibid.**

17. Parrinder, **op. cit.**, p. 109.

18. **Ibid.**, p. 110; Abraham, **op. cit.**, p. 29.

19. **Ibid.**, p. 111.

20. **Ibid.**, p. 112; This position is not new. The Moslem theologian Abd Allah al-Baydawi did not question the Gospel's view that Jesus was crucified, nor did he believe that the Gospels were falsified.

21. G. E. von Grunebaum, **Modern Islam**, N.Y.: Alfred A. Knopf, 1964, p. 8; Parrinder, **op. cit.**, p. 112, 119.

22. Parrinder, **op. cit.,** p. 119; Watt, **Islam...**, p. 260.

23. Sweetman, **op. cit.**, part 1, vol. 1, p. 33.

24. Q 19: 34-35, Abdalati, **op. cit.**, pp. 175-176; Parrinder, **op. cit.**, p. 127.

25. Sweetman, **op. cit.**, part 1, vol. II, p. 30.

26. The best brief exposition of both the classical and modern doctrine of the Trinity is Joseph A. Bracken, **What are they saying about the Trinity?**, N.Y.: Paulist Press, 1979.

27. Sir John Glubb, **The Life and Times of Muhammad**, N.Y.: Stein and Day, 1971, pp. 127-128.

28. Guillaume, **The Life of...**, p. 271.

29 **Ibid.**, p. 272; Glubb, **op. cit.**, p. 295; Brown, **op. cit.**, pp. 20-21. (See: Q 5: 116 "O Jesus, son of Mary, hast thou said unto mankind, "take me and my mother as two gods beside God"?) Parrinder, **op. cit.**, p. 135; Sweetman, **op. cit.**, part 1, vol. 1, p. 32.

30. Guillaume, **The Life of...**, p. 271.

31. Q 9: (entitled Repentance).

32. On this see Ayoub, **op. cit.**, pp. 43-51. For the current Moslem interpretations see Nasr, **op. cit.**, p, 62.

33. Ayoub, **op. cit.**, p. 43.

ABOUT THE AUTHOR

This ia a masterly survey of two of the world's great religions by a master scholar. Dr. A. J Abraham brings his innovative analytical touch to comparative religion in this timeless contribution to the understanding of Islam and Christianity, in an ecumenical perspective.

Dr. Abraham is professor of Semetic civilizations an cultures at New York Institute of Technology. He is a nationally recognized expect on Lebanon and the Arab Near East; he is the author of **Lebanon at Mid-Century, Maronite-Druze Relations in Lebanon 1840-1860: A Prelude to Arab Nationalism,** (University Press of America) and **Lebanon: A State of Siege 1975-1984),** (Wyndham Hall Press).

111